GREYBOY

*Finding Blackness
in a White World*

COLE BROWN

FOREWORD BY ELAINE WELTEROTH
AFTERWORD BY MICHAEL ERIC DYSON

ARCADE PUBLISHING • NEW YORK

First Edition

Arcade Publishing books may be purchased in bulk at special discounts for sales promotion, corporate gifts, fund-raising, or educational purposes. Special editions can also be created to specifications. For details, contact the Special Sales Department, Arcade Publishing, 307 West 36th Street, 11th Floor, New York, NY 10018 or arcade@skyhorsepublishing.com.

Arcade Publishing® is a registered trademark of Skyhorse Publishing, Inc.®, a Delaware corporation.

Visit our website at www.arcadepub.com.

10 9 8 7 6 5 4 3 2

Library of Congress Cataloging-in-Publication Data is available on file.

Cover design by Lineage Digital
Jacket design by Kai Texel
Illustrations by Natalie Johnson

Print ISBN: 978-1-5107-6188-9
Ebook ISBN: 978-1-5107-6189-6

Printed in the United States of America

Contents

FOREWORD

by Elaine Welteroth

The ache for home lives in all of us, the safe place where we can go as we are and not be questioned.

—Maya Angelou, *All God's Children Need Traveling Shoes*

"YOU AREN'T LIKE MOST Black girls." I can still feel my veins fill with adrenaline and my body tense up, preparing itself for the inevitable blow that would come next. *"You're just, like, so . . . articulate."* There it was. The familiar backhanded compliment, like an unwanted gift you've received too many times before. Under different circumstances these could be reflexively classified as Fighting Words, demanding correction through confrontation. But in this context, survival instincts beg you to reconsider.

There I was, a college student working two jobs to put myself through school, peering into the oblivious blue eyes of my employer whose willful ignorance blinded her from seeing me and my intelligence as part of a broader Black community, rich with achievement and, yes, #Blackexcellence. Yet, the painful force of her unexamined prejudice was equaled only by the knowledge that fighting it would be futile—and even more grim, it'd likely leave me unemployed.

We were folding jeans inside a retail store at Arden Fair Mall in Sacramento—a small town that projected itself onto freeway billboards as the proudly diverse metropolitan capital of California. And yet it was the place I witnessed more narrow-mindedness than any other, before or since. Not just from white people who were unacquainted with the notion that Black people indeed spoke "proper" English, but also from Black people who did not always immediately embrace those who did (for reasons rooted in long, menacing histories and divisive tactics designed by oppressors to form deep fissures within the communities of the oppressed).

It is in these jarring moments that our reality seems to divide itself into two, like those split-screen scenes from nineties TV shows. There is the reaction you perform—the diplomatic response they can see and hear and digest without offense. One that allows you to keep your job and, by sheer force of will, eventually becomes just a foggy recollection, a bad dream you try hard to forget over time. Then, there is the internal monologue, replete with the clever clapbacks your conscious mind knew better than to reach for in the heat of the moment, that you will later feed yourself in the mirror and share freely with friends in "safe spaces" fit for unpacking collective rage.

But beyond the bravado and beneath the performative

diplomacy, there is a different voice altogether welling up from the deep chasms between who we are and how we are seen. The voice hidden behind the languages we learn to speak in order to navigate spaces that insist on seeing only parts of us; the parts made most visible through the media's gravely limited projections of us.

This book is written from that voice. The voice that is at once questioning, analyzing, processing, and protesting the world around it—all while earnestly asserting its rightful place within it.

In *Greyboy*, Cole Brown recounts with poignancy not only his search for an integrated Black identity to inhabit, but he sets out on a literary quest to expand the definition of Blackness altogether by teasing out the nuances of existing in-between the identities he and those in his world have been assigned. The essays before you offer beautifully constructed windows into the world of what it means to be, as he describes himself, "a token" in the age of Trump.

As a reader, I found myself smiling and nodding, feeling in my bones the relentless urgency of his mother's warnings each time he leaves her home. I rode the waves of self-betrayal when his belonging at the Black Table was at odds with his similarity to the preppy white kids he grew up with—until, of course, life painfully reveals the lie of sameness we are sold. I laughed along as he fondly recounted the great loves of his life, remembering the days of my own First Love and how hard my young heart had fallen.

As a Black writer all too familiar with occupying white spaces,

I presume one reason I was trusted to write this message to you is that in my book, *More Than Enough: Claiming Space For Who You Are—No Matter What They Say,* I, too, reflect on growing up in a near-constant state of whiteness only to enter adulthood grappling with what it means to find myself more often than not as The Only in room. The token Black friend. The token Black body in the office. Or, as the great Shonda Rhimes cleverly coined us across industry: F.O.D.s (First. Only. Different.).

It is hard to miss the many parallels between our experiences. Though in as many ways as our stories are similar, they diverge primarily on the fundamental characteristics of gender and of a certain socioeconomic privilege. However, even in these seemingly narrow divides between two otherwise similar millennials lies a multitude of nuanced experiences that defy any notion of a monolithic Black identity. As one of the many titles he considered for this book suggests, *Black Boy, Silver Spoon* (which I happened to like), Cole comes from a world of privilege that I wasn't exposed to until well after college. A biracial Black girl who grew up in a working-class white town in California, I did not summer on Martha's Vineyard, nor did I have access to private school education, or the elite Jack and Jill circles he was born into. And yet, I relate deeply to the in-betweenness that Cole writes about.

I have always believed in and championed young voices for their ability to convey something about the world that we might not otherwise see. While his adult life is only just beginning, Cole's writings chart a specific kind of coming of age that explores the arc of coming into one's consciousness and finding a voice of one's own. A voice that, for the first time, strives to articulate itself without compromise, while embracing all the competing parts that make up its whole. This is a story of one young man's journey to develop and define a strong, affirmed Black identity in a world that wanted to define that for him. I, for one, find that to be a very brave and important act.

A Note

To THIS DAY, I wrestle with what to call the thing you're holding, how best to convey what it contains. It isn't a memoir, though it's often about me. It isn't a study, though it's often about others as well. It isn't an anthology, though it has much of that same stitched-together, patchwork appearance. It isn't academic, objective, or authoritative.

What it is is a scrapbook, a collection of stories—some mine, some not. I compiled the stories over hours of formal interviews and years of informal encounters with people like me.

Token: *a member of a minority group included in an otherwise homogeneous set of people.*[1]

These are the collected stories of tokens and the world of white wealth we operate in. In some cases, names and identifying details have been altered. Taken together, I hope the stories provide some insight into the lives we lead.

---

1   Oxford University Press, 2019

My Kind of People

A Black boy on a white porch, flanked by white sand, white people, and a tequila shot (blanco). I'm on vacation. It's spring break *(woot, woot!)* and Juicy J blares in the house behind me, overtop of the palm's rustlings. Three months ago, my college roommate asked me if I'd join him and his family in the Bahamas this year. *Of course, I'll join you and your family in the Bahamas this year, Andrew!* So, earlier this week, I boarded two planes and one speedboat to arrive at the porch I excused myself to moments ago. It is beautiful here, but these pale beaches and swirling seas backdropped a squeamish first dance with paradise.

I jittered with anticipation on day one, floating up to this bucolic scene. A man greeted our group, his dark lips parting for pearly whites. He lassoed us to shore, then he steadied each one who stepped off the vessel. Tattered tee, sandals nearly worn away, slim but defined, with veins snaking his forearms;

his bright smile guided us to shore. *Welcome to the Bahamas! Is it your first time?* As a matter of fact, it is! Island hospitality at its finest. He didn't offer his name and I didn't ask. He shook my hand—four fingers forward, three pumps, wrist uncocked —then gave the others the same. By then, one of his mates had joined us, same dark complexion, but pudgy and stouter. This man sherpa'd our bags into a nearby trunk. I reached for mine, but he shooed me away. *If you insist.* I climbed in and we rolled on, but my gaze followed the men as they trailed off and set-tled back into themselves. I saw the way they mimicked, joked, and nudged; dapped each other up and brought it in for the *real thing.* Such a shame, I thought, that they must stow these selves away when my hosts are near.

Our driver steered us through a shimmering town. It hugged the coastline, its white-blasted cottages made unique by colored shutters. Tourists crawled over the place—jogging, ordering lemonade, checking watches to see if it was time to drink yet. Some waved. An invisible border came and went, and we left the town behind, entering a far shabbier section. I learned later that blow-ins deemed the inhabitants of this island *the Locals.* Their chocolatey skin flagged to which side of the line they be-longed. To the right, an open grill wafted the scent of searing meat, a few brothas sprinkled about its vicinity slumped into plastic chairs. Madame grill master summoned us over with a spatula, calling out something indecipherable, but we ignored her entreaties. Further down the road, a family huddled near each other. A stick-figure of a girl stumbled out to the street playfully as we sputtered past, her mother eyeing us from the patchy shoulder, an infant boy in her arms—unblemished, inky skin like his momma's. Pavement turned to dirt turned to rock and sand as we carved our way through thick bush. When we emerged, an oasis sat on the other side. Home sweet home.

Days bled together, and soon certain features felt familiar. The island is small, so small that a couple days is enough to encounter all the other sun-soakers she harbors. Casual bonds come and go, as vacation pals crawl from the sea, doomed to vanish from memory when the tide of reality returns. Soon after arriving, I became nighttime besties with dozens of these recent migrants. I knew few by name but many by nickname or reputation. I knew all by face. By my calculations, I was the only Black tourist here.

Mostly, Manhattan elites flock here, an entire universe of power and wealth that existed fictitiously as recently as last week.[2] There are Republicans, and white liberals, and women with tastefully done nose jobs, and men with pot bellies that they carry proudly the same way that their grandfathers' grandfathers strode forward from ivory palaces in France and England. There are flowy haircuts, and paisley swimsuits, and buoyant buildings referred to as boats for modesty's sake. One thing there is not? Prosperity for Black folk. Its absence has made me increasingly uncomfortable in a place so starkly divided.

In the course of our daily routines, few forces prove strong enough to lure us out of bed—exploration, flirtation, the beach.

---

2   i.e., *Gossip Girl*. My sister watched it, not me . . . I swear.

Early on, we learned another Georgetown student was around here somewhere, a girl a few years younger who was vacationing in her family's home. We dropped by. Despite its compactness, every new turn on this island revealed hidden glories lovelier than the last. I didn't know the girl well and had never met her folks, but how warm and welcoming they all were to me, a stranger in their midst. *No, I'm fine, thank you. . . . Yes, it is my first time. . . . It has been absolutely wonderful, thank you. . . . No, I'm from Philly actually.*

We toured the grounds. The girl's great-grandmother bought this house. The family provided verbal CliffsNotes on its history. *What year was that again? . . . Oh wow, that far back, huh.* I stilled my responses to nods and *uh-huhs*, not knowing what to contribute. I recalled the portraits of the European military men in the house we stayed in, with whom her great-grandmother may have shared a voyage, traveling with conquest on the brain. I remembered what little Pop had told me of my own great-grandfather, born in 1869, son to a slave. It seemed a downer to mention what my people had been up to at the time.

The tour moved on. Renovations were stalled—the dock or the kitchen or the something or the other. *You wouldn't believe how long it takes to get things done in this place.* A clueless nod in agreement. But then, a pivot to the upside. Gratitude. How fortunate were we all to escape here in the first place? *It's almost hard to believe,* I chimed back in. We took turns praising, in an off-the-cuff sort of way, the utopia we'd happened upon. Others echoed. *It's so . . . authentic!* Unlike vacations past, wasted at other mondo resorts littering the tropics. So grateful to have come upon something so *real.*

My unease leapt to the surface. Two days gone by and I'd scoured the island's beaches and inland alcoves. Where, I wondered, was all this authenticity hiding? Surely not in the forty-four-dollar quesadilla I purchased and ate for lunch, against my better judgment.[3] It couldn't have been the Scottish gin, nor the Swedish tonic. Kitesurfing? Kanye West? Cocaine? Which of these did the Arawak and Caribbean peoples add to our spring break zeitgeist?

Those questions too seemed like downers. I filed them away.

The tour concluded. We said our *see you later's.* No need to make plans. We'd bump into each other one way or another.

Hours slipped away, roasting in the convection heat. *Can you get my back?* We alternated turns shuttling snacks and entertainment from home to seashore. Dinnertime approached. Left with an hour to kill ('round here, poor time is always killed, never spent), Andrew and I ambled along the beach, having fallen behind the rest of our crew. After a near-perfect few days, I was enchanted by the place, just as he warned I would be. Yet a question nagged, left me unsettled. Why was it, I wondered aloud, that people paid such astronomical sums to come *here,* specifically? It's beautiful, of course, special even, but there's a million beautiful, special specks dotting the Atlantic. *Cole, I gotta imagine there's some weird slave-master fetish at work here.*

Ah, so I hadn't lost my mind. Or perhaps we both had.

---

3   No regrets though. 'Twas delish.

Andrew doesn't miss much. That, and his innate inability to give a fuck what people think, is what's drawn me to him since we met freshman year. He's of a waspy caste but regards it with the utmost skepticism, as all should regard the forces that mold them. I've never known him to take this side of life too seriously. But his observation, delivered in a tone so matter-of-fact, cast him off from that community. I questioned if that distance had been earned. What did it say of the man, my close friend, that he could instinctively pinpoint the perversion of those others? Others so similar, in so many ways, to himself?

But soon, a more pressing question intruded: What did it say of me?

If he was right, we were meant to play opposite roles in this production. Colonizer and indigenous. Massa and nigga. Visitor and Local. Yet here I was frolicking about with the gall to *enjoy myself.* My people were out there beyond the dirt road, sandwiched between his family's oasis and the coastline. Must I escape to them? Was each moment spent in the presence of Andrew and his family a betrayal of the Locals, my own distant relations?

The hazy heft of it all stayed with me through the night. It clouded my brow through the dinner, the pregame, and the earliest moments of our time at the local bar, until rounds of tequila shots produced a fog of another kind. But then the question crept back when I woke the next morning, head pounding from it and other influences. I laced up my sneakers to run it off. And that's how I found her.

I ran. Off the porch. Down the dirt. Past the makeshift BBQ joint. Turned along the beach. Dirt. Pavement. Locals. Locals. Tourists. Tourists. Wait. Could it be? A woman, Black even from a distance. Sun-kissed brown skin, only one shade darker than my own, but smooth like putty. A colorful sundress draped her frame and gold trinkets glinted off her wrists—the uniform of the tourist class. She rested comfortably under the arm of her beau, a precisely quaffed white man who himself looked like an Italian model. The two fit so snugly they might melt into each other. I craned my neck to keep my eyes fixed on her, but right-foot, left-foot was complicated in my thoroughly hungover state, and a crack in the pavement sent me tumbling to earth. I shot my eyes up before rising, praying she hadn't noticed, then felt a pang of remorse when indeed, she hadn't. She was unshakeable—totally at ease. Her comfort was captivating.

My savior! My totem! A sign in desperate times. I weighed the wisdom of sprinting over to her right then, the way our people do when few in number. How lovely it would be to learn her name but call her *sista* instead, then to half-jokingly lament our shared, picturesque predicament. I started, but she and her man were fixed in a moment too serene to interrupt. I scurried along, storing her away in my mind, filling the space where confusion recently perched. She, I knew, would be the one to reassure me of my place in this space. This island would bring us back together soon. But even soon would not be soon enough.

The day dragged on after her. The routine of it, for the first time, felt sluggish. Just when I thought I might go mad, there she was again, seated at the restaurant when we entered for dinner. I perked up at the sight of her, tried not to let the others sense my excitement. I chose a seat at the end where I could face her through the meal. She sat just one table away from our group, close enough that I could hear the soothing hum of her voice when she ordered her filet, medium rare, with asparagus on the side instead of mashed potatoes. Where was the quiver of deference I'd heard in my own minor requests? Who knew they allowed substitutions in this joint! She instructed, smiled, laughed, and enchanted freely, bewitching me all along.

I flipped channels constantly between my table and hers. I waited, eager for the wave that would invite me to approach. So many questions bubbled up inside me, and her comfort was at their heart. How was she so at ease in this place? So unlike me; Alice in a tropical rabbit hole.

I fantasized through appetizers, but then the entrees came. The restaurant warmed up. And she removed the silk headscarf that she'd let swing across her forehead and down the nape of her neck. For the first time I saw her hair, close-cut and bleached blonde. I was dumbfounded. The woman I'd so carefully imagined wore her hair natural in tight curls or spun-up dreads. She was a frontline revolutionary. She was going to bridge me to that affirmed Black identity I'd forgotten to fit into my carry-on, abandoned back in DC. The fantasy I'd thrown myself into ever since that morning's stumble lay shattered around my feet.

I reassembled the pieces. I could forgive. We were in this thing together after all. I desperately needed her to remind me who I was. What I was. She wouldn't have to offer much. A thin grin, a knowing nod, a wink, any of those silent notes of solidarity our people had sent each other for centuries. I just knew she had it waiting for me, that those brown eyes were as eager to lock with mine as mine were hers, filling us both with longed-for familiarity.

Servers cleared dinner, served dessert, cleared dessert. Nothing.

The anticipation rose into my throat; I croaked when conversation turned to me. One more chance. Our group stood to leave the restaurant. Party time. I walked as though inching down the gangplank. She needed to recognize me. *Slower now. Arc your path. Come up behind her man. Brush up past her shoulder. Make yourself seen!*

A glance toward, a glance away. Not a trace of recognition, of *we're in this together.* I strode out of her life before she'd ever entered mine.

What the bougie was that!? The floodgates breached, and fury poured in. Who did she think she was? To stand me up, the audacity. It was that white man of hers who had turned her, I reassured myself. She'd strayed too far away, and these white folk had captured her. It wasn't comfort that I saw, it was duplicity. She'd forgotten our common language. Snubbed me? I snubbed her! How could I ever have mistaken her for one of *us*?

We rolled the golf cart down the block and to the bar. I half-collapsed through the doorframe, finding a welcome reprieve in more tequila shots. Plus, other girls from other colleges with spaghetti straps and long eyelashes. *Another round?* Absolutely. *Text me tomorrow!* Will do.

Liquor has a way of driving the scenic route before returning you to your problems. Hours of parodied dance battles passed, and I stepped out to the balcony in need of a reset. I'd caught myself glancing at the entryway every minute since I'd entered. Despite my resignation, some part of me hoped, even expected, that she would burst through the door any moment. She would make a beeline for me, provide some totally rational explanation for the cold shoulder, then we'd go about the business of confiding in one another. *Thank God, I thought I was the only one,* she'd say.

I scanned the street below hoping to find her swaying her way up it. No such luck. But then, just as I was about to plunge back into the drunken fray, I heard a scraping cackle that drew me back to the balcony's edge. It belonged to one of a handful of local guys across the road, loosely assembled, trading low punchlines and loud laughter. I Tom-peeped for a moment longer than was appropriate and smiled along. I spied myself in them too. They reminded me of my boys from back in high school and the rapid-fire shit talk we exchanged. The icy glares they shot at onlookers, the way they crumbled to bent-over belly laughs, only to snap back as though the joy evaporated before their very eyes. I knew the steps to that dance.

I heavy-footed down the stairs, stumbling on the last but catching myself and recovering quickly. I staggered wavily in their direction, not looking at the group, but not *not* looking either. Waiting for one of them to glance and our eyes to catch.

To fire off that head nod that I'd suppressed for days. To be recognized. But nothing. A glance toward. A glance away. I hooked a left for the golf cart, suddenly nervous.

I dropped into the driver's seat and made a show of searching the dash and the gap where the glove box would be. I don't know what I looked for, but it wasn't in my pockets either. Oh well. Now to rise and catch them nonchalantly on the way b—

What the fuck you doing?

That bass could only belong to one of them. A gruff greeting, I assumed, to match their raspy chortles. I perked up, turning with a smile. A dark, round man with sagging jowls and the makings of a beard splattered across his face haphazardly. His cartoon-like features were nearly inviting, until I met those eyes. They were ablaze. The nod he gave was not the one I'd longed for. It signaled *look down*. I followed his eyes to his chin and to the chrome pistol he gripped, pointed at my belly. Sandwiched between his belly and mine so as to remain invisible to any onlooker who might stray onto the balcony and look down.

Whoa, whoa brotha, what's good?

What's good was I'd climbed into the wrong cart. His cart. All these damn things were the same model, I couldn't have been the first to make the mistake. I motormouthed an apology. I even shot off a slight smile, hoping to rekindle the lighthearted man I'd first seen. *Silly, drunk Cole*, my eyes pled.

Get the fuck outta here. Run back upstairs, boy.

The gun was overdone. He seemed to know that. He sheathed it and stepped aside. But *boy* stung, as he intended. If he understood my intention, his expression didn't show it. The rest of his crew collected around us by then, muttering warnings, daring me to respond. I kept my eyes low, moved between them sheepishly.

I followed the man's instructions and clambered up the steps to the happy-go-lucky world above. My time grew fuzzy quickly. More drinks and a few slurred *you wouldn't believe what just happened*s banished the encounter. The night was young and there was still nectar left to be drawn from it.

But the next day the incident returned from exile, when one of the mothers we were traveling with brought it up over lunch. *I heard what happened last night.* At first, it didn't register. But her grim demeanor brought flashes of the moment back. She was referring to the gun, how rattled I must've been in its wake. I laughed that off and assured her I was just fine. *Not the first time I've been threatened with a gun, and compared to the last, this was a breeze.*

That was actually true. It wasn't the gun that threw me; it was the gaze. I've stumbled about this island for days now, praying my people—the other tourist, the Locals—would find something familiar in me. Yet when my eyes finally met theirs, only aggression came back. There was no recognition between me and his crew. No laughing off the mistake and departing as pals. Only the instruction to run along, as though nothing but folly could've pulled me to their orbit in the first place. *Are these my people at all?*

Or actually, more accurately, *am I theirs?*

Now hindsight proffers memories through kaleidoscopic lenses. I recall my arrival to this paradise and the greetings they offered. Those handshakes and smiles were reserved for the visitors who expected as much; reserved for the foreigners who paid for as much. *Can't you see me?* I want to shout back, *Dap me up Goddammit!* I had assumed they ignored me because foreigners were near; now I realized that to them I was the foreigner.

Then the blonde-headed beauty with the brown, baby-oil skin. I was looking for her to supply what I was missing—an assuredness in belonging in this place, in our own bodies. I saw her golden bleached hair as a betrayal of our common ground, but perhaps it was a confirmation. She knew who she was and knew who I wasn't as well. Maybe she saw the duplicity in me that I accused her of. And maybe she was right.

And finally, the macho Local with steel to scare, telling me to run along as if I'd taken a wrong turn when stumbling into his reality. His world, in his mind, was not a place I belonged nor had ever known.

I am forced to confront a frightening truth. Perhaps it's not them, it's me. Perhaps I truly belong to neither side of this world.

I look to one end of it and see Andrew and his family. They have welcomed me in with a warm embrace, fed me, and provided a place to rest my aching head when overwhelmed by the hard work of partying. But I don't feel one with them. I can't. I can never be my travel companions because never in history have I been my travel companions. It would have been unthinkable for my great-grandfather to purchase one of these grand manors, just as it's unthinkable today for most all of my kind to ever see these shores. Despite their graciousness, I resist the space they offer in their midst.

The space that I rush to instead repels me. Am I not Black the way these Bahamians are Black? My instinct and desires say I am, but clearly I'm not in their eyes. I know the compassion, care, and understanding carried in *You good, brotha?* well enough to feel its absence when it's not offered. The bed I rest in and the roof that shields it scream loudly for all to hear where my loyalties lie. The chocolatey woman who creeps into my room midmorning, silently cleaning up my careless mess, or the others who poured and served those very tequilas in beachside bars last night all bear witness, *You are not one of us.* Who am I to claim otherwise?

And then I realize that I am well acquainted with this ambivalence. I've forgotten it for a time, but this was the high school struggle. The middle school struggle. I thought I'd left it there. Filled out my personhood and decided where I landed. Yet here I am, three years, two flights, and one speedboat away, and that same conflict comes creeping back, demanding once again that I stake a claim.

Perhaps there is a third way—to project my ambivalence onto the world, to accept that I am wholly outside of, or equally in-between, these two possibilities. Safe and sensible. I must be both or neither, certainly not one or the other. Perhaps I am my own thing, a token, a greyboy, which is to say a mutt, or one caught in the between place.

But that too wreaks of betrayal. Am I allowing this island's gentle breeze to caress me out of my Blackness? Should I not say it loud, *I'm Black and I'm proud!*? And would the words carry any weight without those around to echo my chant?

Any comfort there is to be had then resides in one final truth: I am not entirely alone. There are others who faced the same dilemma and have found their way to live with it. Perhaps they are my people.

How do you sound, your words, are they
yours? The ghost you see in the mirror, is it really
you, can you swear you are not an imitation greyboy,
can you look right next to you in that chair, and swear,
that the sister you have your hand on is not really
so full of Elizabeth Taylor, Richard Burton is
coming out of her ears.

—Amiri Baraka

NOT REALLY BLACK

CRISSCROSSED ON THE CARPET, cousins gathered 'round, lights low. I sit up near the TV set, within its glow, close enough for Ma to warn against eyes getting fried. There are serious-looking men on the screen conjuring terms I don't understand. The camera cuts between them, each spectacled and stern. I stare eagerly, gleaning what I can from their expressions: not much. Payne steps up—Daddy then—talking through the bushy caterpillar on his lip. I giggle and bubble with glee. The station is tuned to public access television—it's hardly the Oscars—but it beams down from the mountaintop, and my father is what it shows.

So goes my first memory. One of few from the "city" I was born in. Fort Wayne, Indiana; America's first vertebrae. Payne was a big fish in that pond.[4] He was Moby Dick in the kid-

_____

4   Ma was too, but I didn't know that then. She wasn't on TV.

die pool of my mind. He occupied that same screen where the big kids puppeteered Mario and Zelda, slinging eloquence, his suit fitting boxy with room the way suits did in the nineties. The population of my whole young world could be counted on munchkin fingers and toes and each of them was stacked in that living room, captivated.

The image struck me. It had impact. Like most young boys, in the early years, I shuffled myself into Dad's image; placed each atom with intention; took seriously what he seemed to; crossed my legs and wore zip-up ties; walked with my shoulders first. He pressed his temple like Malcolm. I pressed my temple like him.

And all the language that mattered, the language he ping-ponged with pencil pushers by wood paneled desks, I read like a madman to discover it. Dad was a lawyer by training, paid to debate. Tying tot tongues was no grand feat for him. But I studied to contend. Baldwin, Hawking, and Wright while still young. A book a day at peak. One misguided godfather gifted the full Encyclopedia Britannica for an early birthday. So be it. I read that too. The content was of no consequence; the words were my plunder. When aunties asked what I wanted to be when I grew up, I called out *lawyer*, only because *Dad* wasn't a profession.

But it is early in life when other idols push forth for attention, and fathers fade. We relocated. Fast forward a few years from that memory and I'm a Philly boy, reporting each day to Chestnut Hill Academy, an institution full o' Philly boys. My appetite for language grew, and wordsmiths—Langston Hughes,

Missy Elliott, Kanye West—came to contest my father's claim. But I was the exception. Philly boys of my era had a different North Star to chase after, their aspirations personified. He was the prodigal son with David's dimensions and the swagger of Goliath. His name was Allen Iverson; the guard from George- town University was a God for what he did for the city. I can see my classmates now—miniaturized and adrift in a world con- structed by and for our elders. A. I.'s handles told all that we stood a fighting chance. Out on the playground, you might yell *Kobe!* after pulling up from three. And you might wag your fin- ger Mutombo-style after a block. But cross somebody up? That was Iverson. Talk trash and step over him afterward? That was definitely Iverson. Skill wasn't enough; you had to eviscerate to invoke the Almighty.

Iverson was more than an athlete, he was a culture incarnate. Hip-hop culture, basketball culture, Black culture, all of it. A tattooed, rapping, freakishly athletic, rags-to-riches story with a criminal record to boot—a Black, male stereotype you could point to and root for. I was a fan, but not the way that my class- mates were fans. I knew white kids, white kids!, who donned sweatbands, Sharpie tattoos, and blackface just to dress up as Iverson several Halloweens in a row. We were young, mind you, so their ignorance was forgivable (their parents', less so), but that's just how strong a force the Answer was.

Given that introduction to Blackness, no wonder they were unable to recognize my own.

I had barged into a compartmentalized reality. Our slice of

Philly was an insulated, white corner of the world. Iverson, and the circumstances that brought him about, were all the Black they'd ever known. I was a decision to be made. A riddle to be undone. How on earth does one rationalize someone so un-Iverson-like? Rather than alter the primacy of the stereotype, my peers completed more complicated cognitive contortion, dissociating me away entirely: *Oh, Cole's not really Black.*

Chestnut Hill isn't exceedingly unique, and I'm far from alone; we Not Really Black kids are sprinkled about. You can find us in Beverly Hills, and Greenwich, and Buckhead, and the Gold Coast, and the Upper West Side, and all other enclaves of wealth that were formerly forbidden. You can find us in South Orange, and Prince George's County, and Baldwin Hills—enclaves we've carved out ourselves. We are deposited at the Deerfields and the Andovers of the world to learn their ways and speak in their tongues. We're taught to fake the funk until it's hard to remember which funk is our own. And then, when we are good and ready, we infiltrate Harvard's halls, climbing ladders of prestige that were not erected for our purposes.[5]

But being one of the not really Black kids, the self-proclaimed tokens, meant being born into a Black world but growing up in a white one; living life as an exception to the rule. And so, we build coalition communities 'cross borders. Black Greek, and Jack and Jill, and Martha's Vineyard, and *Oh, you're so-and-so's son?!* draw us near enough that few are more than one degree away in adulthood. I found, or was found by, others

---

5   I was rejected from Harvard. Twice. But you get the point.

like me through those collectives established to unite the disparate. With time, we formed a posse. We didn't see each other often, but when circumstances allowed, we congregated, decompressed, and discussed the topics we knew best (everything from Gucci Mane to Goldman Sachs was fair game). We shared in much, but that which was most significant, that which most reliably arose at the Spades table as night turned to dawn, was our perceived greyness.

My white counterparts bestowed *Not Really Black* as a term of endearment, a service of sorts. It was a stamp of approval, an acknowledgement of civility that was their birthright to bequeath. I was to wear it around on my chest like a good Boy Scout and point to it when the uninformed claimed otherwise. In our private school bubble, the kids that *were* really Black were the scholarship kids: the kids who bussed great distances from their neighborhoods to join us each day and had either no ability or no desire to code-switch upon arrival. Their actions, dress, and vernacular had been determined by the environments that shaped them (just like everybody else's). They were wholly other to our lifer classmates. The prep establishment may have sat next to them in math class or fist-bumped them in the locker room, but they were not to be included in weekend birthday parties nor family vacations. Being dubbed Not Really Black by our white counterparts assured us that they knew we were not cut from that same cloth, and therefore might get to see the vacation home in Boca after all.

Looking back, I struggle to recall precise instances of being called to account for my Blackness to a white audience, but not because instances were rare. My greyness was so universally agreed upon. Once a person has been painted in broad strokes, everything else falls underneath.[6]

Others I know didn't allow themselves to become desensitized to the point of detachment. They can still tell you the when and the where; they carry their encounters. Even the most confident of the crew had stories for me.

Sebastian Wells, or Bas, towered over our crew with a domineering presence that was felt physically. The rest of us organized ourselves within his orbit. He's world-renowned. True story: I was once volunteering at my family's school in rural Ethiopia when, totally out of the blue, a visiting American student called out to me, *You look familiar. You must know Mr. DC.* He was talking about Sebastian.

Years later, Bas still remembers receiving this disquieting form of flattery—being labeled Not Really Black by his white counterparts. I wasn't there, but I could join the dots.

The setting was a high school party, and a classic one at that. Some obscure cloudy liquid was on tap—one-part jet fuel, three-parts tropically flavored sugar, and red dye #4. Boys and girls exchanging giggles and goo-goo eyes as the "cool" parents sat upstairs, unseen, yet prepared for duty's call. Bas told me he was chillin', and I know him well enough to know what that meant. He watched casually off to one side like a young Corleone, hood

6   I do remember the girl who waited 'til I went inside to turn to my friends: *I like Cole. He's not too nigger. Wow,* I thought, once they told me, *nigger as an adjective. How inventive.*

up and holding court. I'm sure Sebastian flew above the elated fray; he always has.

That's how Bas socialized; he camped, and kids flowed over in single file or two by two. Some got a chuckle, most didn't, but all were engaged. Sebastian was a benevolent cool kid—never dismissive, just guarded and deliberate beyond his years.

Bas recalls a less familiar face pushing his way into the rotation following time served on its outskirts. The two had seldom interacted—he was the kind of high school acquaintance who is remembered years later only in silhouette, like a shadow puppet, but he caught the references and laughed on cue enough that his presence was accepted, if largely unfelt.

Minutes passed and the chatter was sputtering to a halt; it would be the next group's turn shortly. As kids began to trickle off the same way they had come, having completed their networking for the evening, the faceless man patted Bas on the shoulder:

Ya know, I don't really like Black people, but I like you.

Bas's innards lurched to a halt, sending a single gasp through his lips, agape. *Did he really just say that?* Dude wasn't allowed to see him sweat though. Bas regained his composure in an instant:

Oh, I'm sure that's not true. You don't really dislike Black people, Bas forced through curled lips and warm eyes, before dapping the boy up and sending him on his way.

The words hit home on a couple levels. There was the most obvious: *Fuck you mean you don't like Black people?* Prejudiced certainly, but in a blanket, indiscriminate sort of way. Evenhanded ignorance is somehow more palatable, more easily trivialized away as idiocy.

Then there was the bespoke sting of the assumption that No Name's comment was premised on: *you, Sebastian, are not really Black.* It tinged a nerve that had been rubbed raw by a years-long struggle with identity. But Sebastian didn't handle his addled anxiety the way many testosterone flushed teens would, with balled fists and thorny cries. Even though, mind you, Sebastian would have been uniquely equipped to do so. I don't know it to be the case, but I find it likely that he could have squashed this pest if he wanted to—a fact that might've mattered two Wards over, or a generation earlier.

Primal Power was of little import in this realm of the "civilized." The faceless man had the upper hand despite his anonymity. His very DNA wielded power unmatched by Bas's brawn. Bas was angry, Black, and a man, which brought him dangerously close to the irrecoverable, irredeemable pit of the Angry Black Man. It also brought him to his knees. Sebastian entered a trying state that we tokens are all well familiar with—tearing asunder from the force of two impulses: one to defend his membership in his ethnic tribe, another to avoid the forfeiture of his position in this coveted assemblage. Sebastian opted for the same alternative that I have on countless occasions—suppressing the urge to make a splash to maintain the tranquility of the pond.

I too felt the backhanded sting of Not Really Black. But

somewhere around tenth grade, my particular circumstances gave it a new and revealing twist.

Mama still recalls a woman approaching her in the bleachers. It was a sunny day that sent rays ricocheting off the aluminum seats. Ma recognized her as mother to one of the other Black kids on the track team but couldn't immediately assign her to her progeny. *Look everybody over there talkin', but I told 'em I'ma just come over here and say it—are you an African princess or what?* Ma guffawed and coughed on her spittle a little. She looked up and saw the woman's face hadn't broken—she was serious. Ma peered past her to a group of women sitting at the other end of the bleachers. They were staring back but through side eyes and peripherals.

At home, I hadn't yet washed the track meet off when Ma hollered: *Cole! You going around school telling people you're a prince?!*

Of course, I wasn't.

Some kids had taken two disparate half-truths and Columbo'd Mama to a monarch. On my mother's side, I was, and am, African. Ethiopian to be precise. The home I grew up in was neither bilingual nor exclusively English, but instead somewhere in-between, as were we. I was born in this country and so was Mama, a stark rarity for a full-blooded Ethiopian of her generation. She was put up for adoption and raised in America. Mama's natural mother returned to Addis soon after giving birth and raised her other children across England and Ethiopia. Mama reconnected with them and formed a close relationship long before I entered the frame. From childhood, despite their convoluted histories, visiting Grandma required fourteen-hour flights.

The royal connection wasn't entirely plucked from the ether either. Grandma was the first female senator of the country and the chief hostess under his majesty Haile Selassie I. Today, she traipses around the country like an old rock n' roll guitarist. There is, however, a difference between proximity to power and sitting on the throne.

The separation of those two was conflated because of the second truth—I was different, in many ways, from the other Black kids we'd known. I didn't, I insist, talk, walk, or act white, whatever that means. But I also didn't talk, walk, or act like many of the Black kids at our school. Different experiences breed different characters. As we all do, my classmates sought ways to reconcile their perceptions with understanding. And as we often do, they landed on an explanation that, with the benefit of hindsight, was total absurdity: I was royalty. They wove a *Coming to America* tale, and added Prince of Zamunda to the list of nicknames I was granted in those years.

The sheer ridiculousness of it all blunted the sting of the suggestion. I laughed in concert with others knowing that I was not, nor would I ever be, Prince Akeem. But I never did shake the feeling that behind their comments lurked a question, ever unasked—*you're not like us, you're not like them, so what are you?*

My experience was, admittedly, a particular one. Black America is most often of opaque lineages. Less common is the jumbled up, misinterpretable dataset that comprises mine. *Not*

Really Black in the minds and mouths of Black peers necessarily connoted differently for other tokens.

Amira Rasool was, as many of us are, first-generation upper-middle class. An attorney and a social worker, Amira's parents muscled their way into a better life. By the time I met her on Martha's Vineyard in 2011, the context alone served as evidence of their achievement.

Her parents converted tribulation to prosperity—they made it—but, as is often the case, their relatives hadn't yet arrived. The nuclear unit they formed was a single, flowering branch on a family tree that was largely still working to shake free from hardship. This is the standard, mind you. Few Black families have yet benefitted from the universal uplift that comes with generationally compounded wealth. So, while white wealth creates sovereign islands of delusion, wholly separate from the broader American struggle, Black wealth creates mere jetties. Such was the case for Amira, who puts things in even simpler terms: *everyone still has their hood cousins.*

And Amira felt as though her cousins claimed a monopoly on Blackness that she couldn't share in. Their ridicule was expressed through jest, not ire, but it turned her frame into the prop for a cruel game of tug-of-war. Who she was—really, who she'd been made into—gripped from one side. Where she was from—as distinguished from where she lived, and referenced perhaps, more accurately, as *who* she was from—yanked stiffly from the other. Competition peaked at Thanksgiving.

The extended family congregated at Grandma's house each

year to celebrate the occasion. For Amira's unit, the day meant a trip East from her hometown of South Orange, New Jersey, to Newark—two towns separated by fifteen minutes and a universe.

It was the usual pleasantries when they arrived. *Oh, come over here baby and let me look at you. Have you gotten taller? Look how much you grown!* They joked and laughed and loved the way families are supposed to in those scant, euphoric moments of reunion.

Acrimony crept in with dinner. Grandma's cooking came in the manner that only a Black grandmother's cooking can, which is to say she threw down, stuck her foot in it, and did the damn thing all at once. Enter her home on the third Thursday and dive headlong into an aromatic barrage of brown sugar and sizzling fat. The flavors were an AfAm 101 course. You name it; she had it.

But Amira didn't eat any of it. Well, *almost* any of it. The collards were off limits for starters (she didn't eat pork) and the cornbread and candied yams weren't on the menu either (too much butter and sugar, respectively). The cranberries were all sugar and the mac 'n' cheese was, well, part macaroni and part cheese. She wasn't trying to be picky; she was just trying to be health conscious. But on a day dedicated to glut, her restraint did not go unnoticed. One too many no-thank-yous and snarky jabs flew across the table:

Amira's bougie.

She got that lil white-girl appetite.

It wasn't maligning so much as teasing, but the words ate at her; those interactions caused Amira to question her Blackness most. She'd never considered her diet a question of affiliation. Like anyone, her preferences were learned, not selected. She ate those foods that she'd been exposed to, and they didn't serve collards where she was from. Her family shopped at Whole Foods. They stayed away from the high-fat, high-sodium options because life was healthier that way. Also, of course, because they could. But if her own kin didn't regard her as Black—those who held her same dark blood and could trace it to the same Dark Continent—how could anyone else? How could she?

Amira had entered college by the time she and I became close. She'd knelt at the altars of Coates and Baldwin. Had ideas challenged and debated. The uncertainty she felt as a teenager had hardened into a fierce resolve. It wasn't anger she grew to feel, but disappointment—disappointment in a world that so racialized progress. She saddened with age because what she knew to be simple strides toward betterment, her cousins labeled whiteness.

Having not lived through those bedeviled Thanksgivings, I can be kinder. For her cousins, Blackness was a breathable, familiar thing; they knew it as well as they knew themselves, for it was the Self. And for that reason, they were more greatly affirmed in their understanding, or misunderstanding, of it all than even the white kids we knew were.

There are elements of culture that are irreducibly Black. Language, food, handles on the court: all exist in forms that one can point to and say, *Black people did that.* They are deserving of pride, and defense; they must be protected from further plunder.

But does taking pride in something, in the achievements of those we see as kin, necessarily mean rejecting those who live outside the walls? Must the drawbridge be so resolutely raised? Surely, we can celebrate the fringe kids, those who venture out, expanding the realm we call our own, as boisterously as those who guard the fort and keep the home fires burning.

House Party

Coach's remarks wilted to an end, *Great job tonight boys. See you all to*—I erupted into a sprint, panting and pacing harder than I had throughout practice, leaping knobby patches, taking flight, soaring. My cleated gait turned to tippy-toes when I hit the pavement—slipping would only cost time. I arrived at my car in seconds, gripped the handle, threw it open, yanked it into gear, and jammed my foot onto the pedal in one swift, Tai Chi–like movement, all before he'd formed *mor-row.* I turned to Bradford in the seat next to me:

You think he cared we ran out like that?

It didn't matter.

The two of us quaked with giddy excitement. It was just after 7:00 p.m.; practice had run late. That left us an hour and a half to speed from the Northeast to my home in Chestnut Hill, shower, change, hit the China Store, and get to Erin's house in

Mt. Airy. We were days away from returning to Penn Charter as eleventh graders. That night was our coming out party as upperclassmen; it would set the tone for the rest of the year, and with any luck, all of high school as well.

Every party held high stakes then. Every party held the potential for redefinition. Reputations were built on humid, August nights like those when anticipation ran high. Inevitably, something would happen that night. An event. It would turn heads and arch brows. Whatever it was, it would be laughed about for weeks, even months, to come. The event would be codified to reference words, and those words would be scribbled in 5-point font on desks and balled-up notes. *Remember when . . . ?* Class leaders would sneak it into speeches at all-school meetings, garnering snickers from those in the know, separating them from the rest. And just like that, an anonymous soul would be anointed a *somebody*. Maybe we'd see it go down and laugh along. Maybe, just maybe, we'd *be* it and float across the halls thereafter, knowing we were known. Maybe not. Who knew? Only one thing was certain—miss Erin's and the potential was lost. So when, at the beginning of preseason, the seniors on the soccer team announced our invitation, our reply was emphatic. We belonged there.

Bradford and I spun into my driveway half an hour later with a screech and a skid, inspiring terrifying flashes of the car sliding through the iron fence and right into the pool. No time to dwell on it. I rushed up the stairs, tore off my clothes, and dove into the shower. It hadn't yet warmed, so icy water splashed shock across my chest; I bit my bottom lip as a shriek wrestled for escape. One handful of Axe body wash slathered over my torso and arms and I was done. Then I was in my bedroom tugging black denim to my waist and losing myself in the tangle of a black hoodie. I decelerated for the most important decision: Which kicks? Jordans were the obvious choice. *Ahh, these ones work.*

Now, back to the rush. Brush teeth. Pocket gum. Spray Axe deodorant twice. Okay, maybe thrice. Then twice more for good measure. Holler at Bradford to hurry his ass up. Check, check, check. We were back in the car in minutes and off to the China Store, a corner store in North Philly that, in retrospect, must have had a real name we never bothered to learn (the owners were clearly East Asian, and we were just as clearly ignorant). The store sold alcohol to tweens, luring us on the distant journey. Chestnut Hill, my neighborhood, fell at the city's outermost edges in both geography and attribute. The kids I'd grown up with wouldn't have ventured into the Philly that surrounded the China Store, but Bradford and I were unphased.[7]

Upon arrival, I swerved the car across the opposing traffic lane, ran the tires up over the curb, and threw the shifter into

---

7   During one trip to the China Store, my order was interrupted by the screams of police sirens. I poked my head outside to see flashing lights at both ends, with my car trapped in-between. Naturally, I assumed that after a years-long sting operation, the Feds had finally landed their big fish—me. I sweated it out inside for thirty minutes before digging up the courage to face my fate. I was wrong, of course. Apparently, as I was pulling onto the block, two kids about my age were shooting it out across the street. Somebody told me it was nonfatal, but who knows. It would be a month before I returned. Maybe the kids I'd grown up with had a point after all.

park. I hopped out first, then Bradford followed. We collected ourselves and strutted over, chins high and shoulders swaying. Once inside, we scanned the wall of tallboy cans and malt liquors beyond two inches of bulletproof glass. We knew what we wanted before walking in, of course. We'd fallen asleep the night before and woken up that morning aware of what we wanted, but children preplan that sort of thing. Adults peruse. That's what we were—adults. Finally, I spoke:

Let me get four high gravs.

Huh?

The high grav 40s right there. Let me get four of 'em.

Four Loko, right?

No! 40s! Four!

We continued back and forth, exchanging indecipherable tongues for escalating urgency, until at long last, through heightened volume and pseudo sign language, we came to an understanding. Bradford and I jetted out of there, fist bumping as we scurried—a toast to our victory.

The treasure trove we brought to Erin's was 160 ounces of liquid gold—one for me and two for Bradford, plus an extra, just in case. Still racing, we dashed to her door and our bright, new futures beyond it. But the excitement couldn't last. With time, our adrenaline drained. Our heart rates slowed, and our vision broadened beyond its pinhole view. We checked the place out, struggling to comprehend that her living room was not, in fact, the mountaintop.

Disappointment came with increasing frequency then. I

pined for those events, yet I discovered mostly awkwardness upon arrival. We were the only Black kids there. I knew before I entered that the rest of our crew either wasn't invited or wouldn't come, and more the former than the latter, but their absence left an icy vulnerability. It was strange. Only months before, the partygoers *were* my crew. But as high school wound on, the tectonic plates below began a drift. At Erin's, an ocean stretched between us.

I yearned to be Bradford then. He floated around the room on a gust of laughter and high energy. He was a goofball who played on the lacrosse team with those kids and they all loved him. He and I knew it to be a strange kind of love, a distant and unfamiliar sort, which in truth, was not a love at all. *Oh, I love Bradford!*—words intended to speak volumes more about the subject than the object or the relationship between the two. But no one cared. He was popular.

The party crept along, snug like a too-tight turtleneck. I moseyed to and fro, itchy. Eventually, the crescendo neared. I mingled in the living room, sipping my 40, bouncing between groups, when a call rang out, *Cops!* I spun in search of Bradford, whose eyes locked with mine from across the room.

This, we knew well. It sounded the hour so many agonized over—my Ma, his parents, my Pop, his brothers—they'd all pleaded and cautioned. I wore all-black for a reason. The two of us had run drills, learned to prepare in advance. We'd dash out the back door and dive under the cover of night, then pick a leafy tree to squat and wait. We'd circle back for my car, but not

until chirps and purrs were all that cut through the night's still-
ness. We'd done it before. We'd reminisce soon, under that tree,
they thought they had us!, but laughter was for later. Warnings
had fixed fear in our bellies. It bubbled up from deep, instinctively. It shot the starting gun, told us to break like a banshee
and not turn back 'til we found our punchline on the other side
of safe and sound.

I met Bradford at the back door only to peer out and see
flashlights shining through the window. *Shit!* We dashed off
to another side door, lights there too. Then another. Then the
first-floor windows. The glow trailed us, glares staring back,
barring each escape route. Bradford moved for the foyer.

Follow me!

My heart rhythmed a staccato into my ribs as I bounded to
the second floor. I was barely able to keep up with Bradford,
and I just caught him as he dove into a bedroom on the left. He
made a move for the closet, only to find four of the older girls
hiding in it.

Can we jump in here with you guys?

No!

It was a huge closet for four not-so-huge girls, but they
swung the door shut before he could appeal. So much for loving
Bradford. There was only one option left and we moved for it
simultaneously. I leapt across the bedroom to the second-story
window and tugged for it to open. After some jiggling, it came
loose, and I propped it with my elbow as Bradford stretched his
leg through the opening. We'd jump and pray.

As we'd scrambled frantically, door to door, the hovering lights outside entered. As we'd dashed up the stairs, they cleared the first floor. Then they stalked our trail. I'd forgotten to close the bedroom door. When the officers reached the hallway, they found bandits on the verge of escape. A hand—meaty with sausaged digits—materialized from my periphery. It reached around my head, grabbed Bradford by the neck, and yanked him to the ground. Before I could turn around, I too had been yanked, and the carpet rushed in to greet my chin with a thud. Then the hand wrapped itself around its Glock and tugged the weapon from its holster. It locked us in its sights. The gun lingered above our heads, but its weight pancaked us to the floor. I wheezed. My life, the very breath in my lungs, felt heavy, borrowed, and due. There was another call:

Hey guys, we got two in here. Come on in.

The hand had discovered the closet dwellers too—they were directed, not snatched. They sat on the bed behind us distraught, yet comfortable, squeaking silly things they'd heard on TV like, *We have rights!* We all knew which two had got got—the two spreadeagle, face down on the carpet.

Life before Erin's was a game of decades—choices made today that I likely wouldn't be called to account for at an unspecified later date. That's childhood for the fortunate. The floor was a matter of seconds and centimeters, tiptoeing a line so fine as to be nearly nonexistent. I didn't know the rules to this game. I was terrified, but more than that I was confused—trembling, short-circuiting, and struggling to compute.

Bradford was as new to this as me, yet he maintained control. He wasn't struck by its force, nor shocked into inaction. When Cop #2 finally relaxed his trigger finger and turned his back to us, Bradford whispered to me:

Cole, don't tell him your real name. We have to hide our IDs so our parents don't find out.

So sensible. At sixteen, if I ended up drunk and dead at a house party, Ma would've killed me.

Okay. Where?

He paused.

Our butts. . . . We have to hide them in our butts.

What?!

I yelped and immediately shot my glance upward to see if the cops had noticed the outburst. They hadn't. I looked back to Bradford, his thin-slitted stare insisting I take this seriously. I nodded in unsteady submission.

I rose several minutes later at the officer's command with a knot in my stomach and three forms of identification between my cheeks. We waddled behind them through the hallway and back down the steps to the living room where they'd gathered the partygoers, directing us to sit quietly and await instruction, which we did. Some more comfortably than others. The officers buzzed back and forth. Every few minutes they'd add a classmate to their collection. Then, closets cleared, they stopped searching, and the lot of them moved to the kitchen to confer, leaving one behind—a silent overseer. We strained to hear their whispery exchange. Time slugged on. Still on edge, it felt an odd relief when two of the conferees finally reentered the room:

Whose parents are lawyers or judges in Philly?

Half the room raised its hands and I scanned the group as they did. I'd been knotted and taut for an hour by then. For the first time, I let out a silent sigh. Then the other cop chimed in:

And how about uncles and aunts? Who has close friends that're lawyers or judges in Philly?

I shot my hand up, as did the others that'd resisted previously. Cop #1 shot Cop #2 a glance, and they retreated back to the kitchen and their colleagues; but by then, everyone in the room knew what came next. We knew that more than a few of the families represented in that room could bring down unparalleled hell on the careers of these cops, and that some would delight in doing so. It appeared the cops were developing an appreciation for that as well. They returned moments later with an announcement:

All right, we're going to be nice tonight. All the drivers get in a line. You can leave with whoever you came with.

I exhaled and rolled to a stand. I'd live to jeopardize my future another day. I shuffled to the back of the line and watched as, one by one, kids nodded along to an officer's parting words, pointed to their passengers, and skipped out the front door, unscathed. I shot a look to Bradford that said, *that was close, but we made it, baby.* He lifted a soul fist in return.

I stood third from the front when my final obstacle shifted into view. The officer blocking the doorway wasn't just lecturing, he was checking driver's licenses. Mine was still marinating. *Next!* What to do? I would say I lost mine. But what if they don't let me leave? Too late to turn back now. *Next!* I inched forward.

License.

I peered down at the calloused palm. No choice. I stretched my reach as though fishing in my back pocket, plucked the ID from its crevice, and placed it in the man's hand. The gallery behind me stirred and snickered at the sight. It took him a moment, but a snort from one of his partners got him there:

Seriously kid? Get the fuck out of here.

I did just that.

Years have massaged away the terror and bewilderment of that night. The embarrassment, too, evaporated. The humor and barely-there reminiscences are all that remain. Yet, each time the story arises, once the laughter subsides, I remember that if privilege had a voice, it would sound like our cackles. The episode was token life boiled down to precious few flashes. We escaped tragedy—more than can be said for so many in our position—a happy ending due entirely to the affluent context in which it occurred.

When school came Monday, tales of the party dripped off lips like snuff. But the excitement of having been *there*, of knowing the punchlines and how they'd land, was not so sweet. Like the party itself, the insider-ism that followed fell short of the pie I'd baked in the sky. In the hallways, I recounted the story with the pacing of a joke, yet angered when the bros laughed along. It felt an uncomfortable approximation of minstrelsy. My disorientation needed space for oxygen and understanding.

The shag pattern emblazoned briefly on my face served as a macabre notice that affluence alone could not be relied upon as sufficient cover when stakes were highest—that my trajectory would be colored by vulnerability at all times and that to forget that fact would be to walk naked and blindfolded through the battlefield. Privilege delivered me from the brink that pigment pushed me toward.

*I feel most colored when I am thrown against
a sharp white background.*

—Zora Neale Hurston

The Black Table

IT'S TOO GODDAMN EARLY for this shit—was the only thought produced at 7:30 a.m. as I rolled my mother's car into the senior lot. I wrung myself out before throwing open the door and swinging to the gravel below. It was Martin Luther King Day and I was deep in the throes of senioritis. The disdain I felt was just one of the many symptoms of my recently contracted condition (others included an inflated sense of self, increased libido, and acute aloofness). Shortly before I arrived as a new student that year, CHA's administration replaced the more common day of service with a program of facilitated discussions on diversity and pluralism. The powers that be deemed it Multicultural Day. Or was it Diversity Day? Maybe We-White-Folks-Get-the-Rest-of-the-Year Day? I can't remember. Whatever they called it, it was time retooled for awkward pauses and white guilt.

On their program of events, a movie screening claimed the

morning hours. In the auditorium, lights dim, its title screen appeared: *The Prep School Negro*, it read. The filmmaker himself appeared with it—a round-faced brotha, thin goatee, and glasses, with one of those wool-brimmed hats that delivery boys wore in 1920s England. He looked like he'd smell of coffee shops.

He was once one of those, we learned—a prep school Negro—and had returned to the hallowed grounds of his induction, curious what'd changed since his departure. He interviewed high schoolers on the topics you'd expect: class, relationships, and the struggle to fit in. In short order, he turned to a topic only an insider would consider—lunch. A brown-skinned girl with glossy, straight-as-a-board bangs sobbed while describing feeling unwelcomed at the table where all the other Black kids sat. Moments before, the movie had cut to that same girl standing on the front porch of a grand stone manor asking her close friends whether they'd rather, *[sing] here, or in the piano room?* A deep voice oozed next—another brown-skinned girl with a purple hijab arcing precisely just above her eyebrows. She didn't have the same uncertain quiver: *All the people that play football sit together. All the other white people sit together. So why can't we all sit together?*

While they spoke, the screen flashed images of a high school, a cafeteria, and a lunch table that could have been my high school, cafeteria, and lunch table. I was so engrossed in their interviews that a few long moments passed before I realized that, in fact, they *were* my high school, cafeteria, and lunch table. The exact table I sat at everyday while at Penn Charter was being presented as a case study on the institution of the Black Table in private schools. The documentary was apparently filmed just before I'd entered high school, which is why I was slow to recognize the characters. But when it hit me, it did so literally—I nearly fell over in my chair.

—————

My parents and I decided I should leave Chestnut Hill Academy in seventh grade, well before we knew where to head to next. I was all topsy-turvied in myself that last year at CHA and in need of a reset. I lobbied for a local public school. My friends there had a long leash to play with, and lore of their exploits spread far and wide. I wanted in. I couldn't tell the parents this of course, so I cloaked my motives as best I could.

But Dad, it'll be a new experience.

Mom, think of all the money it'll save the family!

My father heard me out, even seemed to buy it to an extent. Ma saw through the act and told me to try again.

Eventually, we settled on William Penn Charter. The storied school had a gold-plated matriculation list, Quaker morals to lean on and, relatively speaking, a diverse student body. Its administrators cherry-picked pupils from a great distance in all directions, then worked hard to craft the utopia they imagined possible. But the differences brewing beneath the Black Table sat outside their jurisdiction. The administration's efforts ensured we'd share hallways but weren't enough to merge our realities. The student body took those efforts and spat them back, then self-segregated and filed two by two to our corners—a tradition that worked marvelously well for me. I trotted to our little ghetto each day beaming, thrilled with what I discovered there.

What is this Black Table of which you speak, you ask? For its citizens, it was a community within a community, a fortress under siege, a safe harbor where co-conspirators plotted sedition and subversion. It was the vision of Soul City, NC, where disparate minorities pilgrimed to be converted into a cohesive *only*. Yes, it was a lunch table, but it was also much more. It was identity. *We* were the Black Table—a label we did not coin but embraced each time it broke loose from the lips of our white counterparts. And in that way we crafted an illusion of control, nuzzling out a place of our own amid the chaos. It was a haven for us few students of color to congregate in both solitariness and solidarity and receive a much-needed dose of similarity before braving the hallways once more.

The Black Table was not, however, the same shining beacon of escapism for all tokens, and for a time I avoided its embrace. It posed a difficult dilemma: whether or not to publicly embrace our racial identity. Both options would have consequences. Choosing to stray meant risking reclassification as raceless, if not altogether white, by most all of our peers. Those raceless ones were a hot topic of conversation at the Black Table. Why did they stroll on? Were they trying to pass as something they could never be? Did they think they were better than us?

The white kids didn't know what to make of them either.

These strays forfeited their membership to the tribe and left behind the protections it endowed. Their choice ushered in vulnerabilities. They were on their own when discomfort came. Say if, for instance, while sitting at lunch one afternoon, one of these raceless tokens accidentally bumped elbows with the white student next to him causing that student to spill his cup of whatever, and if in response, another white student exclaimed, *Nigga, you crazy!* in a mammy-style voice from across the table, this token would have little choice but to grit his teeth and chuckle along. Keeping it real would come with a possibility of total ostracization that was too large a risk to bear.

That'd become my reality early on in high school. I clung to a crew I'd grown close to when I first arrived at Penn Charter. Well-meaning, middle-class, suburban, white guys seeing in me, for the first time, a Black boy they called *friend.* By and large, they were recruits brought in to join our high-powered lacrosse team.

To the extent that *white culture* exists, the world of lacrosse was its cornerstone with its own vernacular and dress. Its zealots rocked flowy blonde locks and a pastel-colored uniform. Just as Texas has football, Northeastern private schools have lacrosse. At Penn Charter, theirs was the dominant culture. I tried to fit that mold for a time. Out were the hip-hop tees and graphic hoodies. In were polos, Air Maxes, mid-calf socks, and *bro*. Eighth grade went smoothly enough.

But as high school approached, so too did a tide of transformation.

An ever-widening chasm stretched between myself and The Lax Bros and Broettes I'd grown close to. High school introduced a new social hierarchy that we all clambered to ascend. Though it wasn't said explicitly, amid the mad dash for girls and popularity, I'd become dead weight. Weekend invitations trickled away. In school, I became the butt of an increasing number of jokes. And when those jokes turned racial, gone were the previous pretenses and awkward pauses. When *nigga* slipped out, or disparaging comments about the Black boys and girls around us, few thought to acknowledge how I may hear their words differently. By the middle of ninth grade, after a few months of uneasy tiptoeing in and out of their circles, I was prepared to call the Black Table my new lunchtime home. I made my move in winter. The running joke that week was that Cole had gone back to Africa.[8] Seriously.

At Penn Charter, the Black Table was comprised almost exclusively of kids who had arrived since seventh grade. Most were on scholarship, many were athletes, few had fathers at home, and only one other one lived in a Chestnut Hill-ish neighborhood. Daryl Worley, Drizzy, or simply D, was the best athlete in the city and the de facto leader of our pack. D came from the roughest part of Norf (no, not *North*) Philly but seldom bothered to flex his street credentials; we knew he'd seen some shit. Athletics became his escape route, transforming him first to a Mountaineer, then to a Panther, a Raider, and a Cowboy in due time. We recognized his potential long before he got rich

8   An impressive reference in its own right. They for damn sure weren't taught Marcus Garvey in history class.

off acrobatics. D was a braggard, but beneath the showmanship he had a subtle self-assuredness that let you know he wasn't all bluster. Or maybe not. We so emulated him that it's difficult to discern whether I still view his fifteen-year-old self with fourteen-year-old eyes. At any rate, the ladies loved him. Little else mattered after that.

Bradford had a seat there. He was very much in-but-not-of the private school system, as he had attended prep schools since his earliest days but was re-inducted into distinctly Black family dynamics each day when he returned home. Bradford was candy cane and cotton stuffing trapped in a domineering frame, yet years spent as third in a line of troublemaking brothers bestowed street smarts he couldn't possibly have picked up at Penn Charter. He transferred from CHA the year after I did and, like me, laid first roots across the cafeteria. I can't now remember which of us was the first to emigrate, but the other soon followed.

Devon Smith sat two seats to my right. On paper, we had similar backgrounds; Devon was the son of two accomplished lawyers and grew up in a well-to-do Philadelphia suburb. He followed his father's footsteps to Morehouse after leaving Penn Charter and, following time spent with Goldman Sachs and Blackstone, has a much clearer idea of what success will look like in adulthood than the rest of us do. Devon and I chased each other around through enough family vacations and weekend house parties that *Devon-and-Cole* is still treated as a single, hyphenated moniker by many.

These guys, and a few I haven't mentioned (some with far less happy endings), comprised what others referred to as the Black Table, but what we fondly dubbed *La Familia*, after a lengthy debate over who the Don was one Autumn afternoon. 11:15 a.m. was the hour of revolution—time for us to usurp control of our whereabouts, leaving behind the New Deal, and Pythagoras, and *Hola, me llamo Cole* to discuss the things that really mattered. With each topic posed, we quarreled as though we were mining for precious jewels.

Who better, J. Cole or Kendrick?

Yeah, but Kendrick snapped on "Control."

Don't forget about Meek nigga!

Would you shoot a nigga if . . . ? Okay, but what if he . . . ?

You think Sarah would fuck a Black guy?

How 'bout Ally? Nicole? Taylor? Sophie? Sabrina? Lauren? Julie? Mary? Maddie?

Not yo ugly ass.

What the fuck we doing tonight?

We drinkin'?

Why not?

You lettin' that cop disrespect you?

Oh, shut up nigga, you ain't doing shit. . . .

Each lunch was a battle of the minds where witty jabs were rewarded with nodding heads and cackling howls. The victors were granted the spoils of credence and dap; the defeated were left to brood through fourth period. It was a familiar game; one that I had trained for, even. But the reps I put in with Dad for all those years proved to be of little use here. The language I'd picked up while paging through Britannica was a source of insecurity among this new crew. Like Amira, I had cousins who teased me too—most often, for the way I spoke—but they were all in West Virginia and Indiana; I wrote their slights off as differences in geography rather than identity. When the guys at the Black Table told me I talked white, I was left without a life raft to hold onto. I was welcomed to the table that first day, but their respect, and certainly their trust and affection, were privileges I'd have to earn. And to do so, I'd have to keep up.

Let me hol' that jawn.

I'ma run you a dub for it, g.

Naw nigga you drawlin'. I'm straight.

This was the vocabulary lesson I'd missed. I was light-years behind, but I caught up quickly. Drawlin' was no different from trippin' and a dub was twenty dollars. Jawn was everything else, anything under the sun. I gained fluency and soon the dialect became second nature. It was a blessing—I'd shed the verbiage that marked my wackness. I learned to swat back and, when presented with enough gumption, my points were heard in earnest. It wasn't long after that that they incorporated me into nights out, and *Mama Brown* became ubiquitous terminology.

To say that our time, hunched over ham hoagies and Hi-C, brought us together would be a tragic short selling of what I found there. We were brothers—each other's keepers—at least we said as much, and when they told me they'd be there for me 'til the end, I believed them. Once inducted, all manner of personal transgression could be forgiven, save one. Disloyalty converted you to castaway.

The conversations we had around that table weren't often profound, and in retrospect they reeked an inescapable odor of toxic hypermasculinity, but they were admirably unfiltered. The debates were an honest reflection of what we were—a bunch of kids trying to figure this world, and our place in it, the hell out.

It was among these young men that I formed my own conceptions of manhood and Blackness. They taught me the lessons that my parents, out of some perceived awkwardness or distance, never could have. In our own way, we covered all that mattered—religion and politics, fatherhood and responsibility, dating and depression. We covered and recovered sex until it only made sense to try something new on for size. And when we tired of that, we returned to sex again.

When a topic landed on the table, a sizeable swath of Black America called out in response. Most of the brothas had had the benefit of cementing their ideals over a lifetime spent as members of the majority in Black neighborhoods. They spoke with conviction even, or perhaps especially, on that which they knew least about. I soaked all their words in, weighing the views of the devout Muslims at the table against those of the Baptists, Catholics, and Agnostics. I balanced light-skinned against dark and brown, and I measured hood enlightenment opposite working-class wisdom. Each day, I arrived at some middle ground to stand on and added it to my own brand of Black. My friends were not mentors so much as they were haberdashers, weaving together my sense of Blackness and finally dealing me the pelt that I slid onto my body after so many years of uncertainty.

The Black Table was so transformational in my own life that it was difficult for some years for me to see the institution as anything but a force for good. And then I talked to Taryn Wright, for whom the advantages of the Black Table were not always so clear-cut.

Plainly speaking, it would be woefully self-aggrandizing for me to call Penn Charter an elite school and then use the same pathetically inadequate term to describe the school that Taryn attended. Hers was one of those New Jersey boarding schools that you see in the movies—boys and girls with utterly tussle-able blond hair in the Gryffindor striped ties and *Dead Poets Society* blazers scampering around while Boccherini's "String Quintet in E" plays overhead—she'd argue that that's an antiquated image of the prep school, but really. . . . It has its own eighteen-hole golf course. Yes, a fucking golf course.

Taryn goes hot 'n' cold remembering her days navigating the lunchroom jungle. She came to the school as a tenth grader, stick thin and button-nosed with skin like hickory. Taryn was one of the lucky ones early on. She avoided the lonesome new-girl phase, standing tray-in-hand by the register and scanning for a small plot of unclaimed territory. She befriended two Black classmates during her first days at the school and the three congealed quickly. The Black Table provided her harborage. She spent those first few months chatting through lunch with those partners in crime—her best, and only, friends. Inevitably though, that would change. She was a kind, easily liked girl. She played soccer in the fall and ran track through spring. It was only a matter of time before new friends of all colors flocked. The expansion complicated her relationship with the Black Table and its residents.

Her *new* new friends—blond and brunette and white and Hispanic—tugged her elsewhere. She poked her pinky toe into betrayal, stealing away from the Black Table to join the others one afternoon, returning the next to check how her transgression had been received. Again, Taryn was one of the lucky ones. Both crews were levelheaded and generous (something that can't always be said about the interpersonal exchanges of high school girls). She agonized over a decision they apparently cared little about. Neither expected to monopolize her time. But, she thought, if only the groups could come together, then there wouldn't be a choice to be made at all.

Taryn planted a foot in each circle and filled the space between with uncertainty—how to bring these crews together? She commenced a new routine with her peers. She'd enter the cafeteria chittering alongside a classmate from third-period English. They'd stand in line together. They'd pick out meals and swipe cards together. And then they'd act out their respective parts. Taryn first:

Want to come sit with us today?

Majority member followed with various improvised versions of a similar sentiment:

Oh, I don't think I can sit there.

Or

Oh, I don't know if I'm allowed to sit there.

Or

I think I'm going to go to my normal table, I think.

Without exception, Taryn's newest friends felt unwelcome at the Black Table. Which is not to say they *were* unwelcomed at the Black Table. Taryn herself thought the hostility they felt was projection, that the barriers they sensed were self-imposed. She remembers how the table got its name, *It's not like it's actually the Black Table. We wouldn't call it that. They would call it that, ya know, the people who didn't sit there.*

Eventually Taryn forfeited her hopeless crusade of integration. Over time, she inched closer to her newest friends, the white ones, and spent fewer afternoons among her comrades at the Black Table. She still went, though less frequently, and spent much of high school straddling that phantom borderline that had all the divisionary power of concrete and steel beams.

Another of my token cohort, Maya Holder, attended a prep school just outside of DC that was like Taryn's in stature but sadly lacking in golf facilities. The all-girls student body had to make do with a riding program instead. She had similarly awkward encounters with white friends who came to her in her role as official liaison to the citizenry of Negroville:

Maya, why do all the Black people sit together?

To her, the answer was simple:

Why do you guys all sit together? You can identify with one another.

I read her words on plain paper and chuckle, hearing them in her voice. Maya aged with an edge and reminisces with a bite. She's wonderful, of course, just not warm and fuzzy, and when speaking to her, one senses a limit to her cordiality that would be unwise to push past. I did not know her in our youngest days, but I'm told she wasn't always this way. She had to grow into herself just like the rest of us. Imagining her younger self, I must wonder if she really always met the majoritarians' inquiries with strength, or if insecurity ever made her mousy. By her own admission they were some of her closest friends, and belonging can be a fickle fix. I take her words at face value. She says she didn't shrink from the moment, so she didn't shrink from the moment. But I certainly wouldn't have blamed her if she did.

Taryn and Maya both faced the challenges of maintaining their relationships across tribes that maintained all the distance to be had. Mixed loyalties required a different sort of negotiating that I was fortunate to avoid—constantly shuffling from one to the other, regularly translating across party lines. There was, however, another route they could've taken to circumvent this balancing act—assimilation. It wasn't their desired path nor mine, but I've seen how it too can work. I watched my sister claim it for herself.

If not for our parents swearing that it is not in fact the case, I might think Faith and I were plucked at random from the two ends of the galaxy. We're that different. Faith was into the arts growing up; I was an athlete. Faith works out the details; I'm a big picture guy. Faith's emotions guide her; I'm mostly logic.

People tell me that Faith is both boisterous and warm; she's always known how to work a room. Those same people tell me I come off as too serious, or worse yet, arrogant. But Faith has my paternal grandmother's rounded face and my mother's everything else, so if one of us is adopted, it ain't her.

We were at odds throughout childhood, likely due to all that difference. She is four years my junior, right in the sweet spot of sibling annoyance. We exchanged more nasty words and stomped-on steps than I could even begin to count today. But our relationship changed course days before I began ninth grade. That's when Dad left. I stowed away my own feelings of abandonment and filled the crater he'd left in me with the many new duties I had toward her. She wrote me a note on my eighteenth birthday. It said I'd become a second father to her. Once she exited the room, the tears I shed loosed pride and heartache in equal measures. We drew closer still once I left for college; sometimes distance has that effect. She's damn-near grown now, and our relationship is quickly approaching parity, but I am still as fiercely protective an older brother as I ever have been, much to her chagrin.

The community we shared was the only one near enough for Faith to cling to, and it shaped her more than it did me. Faith was a lifer at Springside, CHA's neighboring sister school. She arrived there at age four and could not be convinced to part ways with it (save for a brief, semester-long experiment in the Upper East Side of Manhattan that ended nearly as quickly as it began). Chestnut Hill was a world, her world; she backstroked through its cobbled streets. The friends who stuck with her were the ones she made at Friday night skate at the local ice rink. And while sneaking watery beers after nightfall on the fifth hole of the golf course. And during springtime strolls up Germantown Avenue with its quaint quilt shop and co-op grocer. She slumber-partied with Chestnut Hill friends and petted Chestnut Hill dogs in Chestnut Hill dens and, as logic would have it, soon became a Chestnut Hiller herself. (She would rail against that most unholy epithet today, but back then, the shoe fit.)

When lunchtime came, the choice, to the extent that one existed at all, was simple. Springside had resegregated as Penn Charter had. Faith tells me her Black classmates claimed a corner and huddled close. She only waved to them from yonder. Not unlike Taryn's majoritarian mates, Faith felt estranged, like a trespasser in their midst. She remembers being labeled bougie and the snickers that emanated when she turned to set her tray elsewhere. She felt unwelcome. She felt judged. Having not spoken to the Corner kids, it's impossible today to parse reality from projection—whether she was *actually* unwelcome, or her insecurities grew ghosts. Either way, that which she sensed simplified the choice—friends or others. She made her decision subconsciously and at a young age, which isn't really a decision at all. She sat with her friends.

There were consequences to the path she didn't choose, positive and otherwise. Faith forged lifelong bonds with likeminded girls—girls who spent enough time in our TV room to become like sisters themselves. I'm sure I'll watch from the pews soon as one or two of those girls flank Faith on her wedding day. And I suppose to the extent that can be expected, they *got it.* But not fully. Not like other Black girls would've. Faith has withstood the same slights on hair and hips that are known to most all Black women, yet she's rarely had a support system to trade war stories with, has rarely had peers to confirm her sanity. She's been popular, with friend groups stretching into the dozens, but skin-thickening and pride-gulping produce their own strain of isolation:

I still feel that there are issues that come up that I know for a fact my friends won't understand. I've taken a 'pick your battles' and 'it's not worth it' sort of attitude with it rather than a confrontational one. But honestly, it goes both ways because I feel like there are issues that would come up within an all-Black setting that I would feel differently and alone on. . . .

She faced a uniquely token dilemma. Both spaces would've been permissible and thus neither fit snugly. Other kids saw identical and wholly other. They made the predictable choice. Our choice was not the same. Lunchtime for us was a decision at the margin.

On the one hand were our white peers. We'd known them longest and shared in most. But white supremacy is not spontaneously born, and the seedlings of that grisly tree were well in bloom by the time we reached high school. On the other hand were our Black peers, with whom we shared less in the way of life's markers, save for that which was most outwardly defining.

Alignment with one almost assuredly meant an awkward two-step away from the other.

Those constant difficult choices made the lunchroom a microcosm of token life. We trained—learned and refined the survival strategies we'd need. Shit talking. Politicking. Code-switching. The tightrope we toed stretched into adulthood; lunchtime taught us our balance. Each meal demanded we shuffle into an identity, then broadcast our choice widely for all to see. And all to judge.

But that choice is nothing new. It is generational. It is historical. It has defined life for those Not Really Blacks since the birth of Uncle Tom, and the house niggers before him. Scores confronted the same dynamics we negotiated. Long before we appeared, our foremothers and forefathers created spaces for us to inhabit free from the pressure to choose. Token tables. There, Black could be whatever we wanted it to be; whatever we were. A decade before we parked our butts at the Black Table, our parents, presaging the challenges we'd face, funneled us through the institutions erected by our forebears.

Church came first. Mama and Dad dragged us to Sunday school in the chapel's basement—zip-up ties and ear pinches whenever I dozed. I learned the Gospel through coloring books with strangers. I would have renounced all beliefs then and there if it meant I could be spared a minute in the clutches of the church bowels. When class eventually ended we sped home to un-noose me and then, once a month, move on to the next phase. Dad—lucky Dad—stayed home. Mama and the children drove off to token primary school—the activities of Jack and Jill of America.

On a January day in 1938, Marion Turner Stubbs Thomas founded Jack and Jill in Philadelphia with twenty other women. Thomas was then a concert pianist, daughter of the city's first Black board of education member, and soon-to-be twice widowed to doctors—a token. Black and white photographs show a woman who can't clearly be labeled either. She sought to counter the ills of oppression with community. She wove together a village that could nourish the curiosities of Black children in a nation that fought to see them go hungry. Originally, it was a vehicle for assimilation, educating the highest reaches of Black society, propelling them to perpetuate their parents' position. It proved interest existed elsewhere: ten chapters had been established by the time of incorporation in 1946. Membership fell in the sixties as Black Power arose. Jack and Jill adjusted. The movement forced modernization. The group I joined at the turn of the century inculcated cultural appreciation. It celebrated Kwanzaa and toured civil rights sites. And it'd gone national.

Jack and Jill gathered together the tokens sparingly sprinkled at predominately white schools across the city. There were ski trips and etiquette classes and art museums and service projects. Come high school, there were national conferences and region-wide parties. I detested it when young, the way a child views all things compulsory as the yoke. Mama insisted I stick with it, *you'll thank me when you're older*. By high school, I started to come around. Mama was right. Those parties were lit. More important, I'd befriended Black folk from Boston to DC, created a Black network of my own that, while not close-to-home, would move with me through life. The token crew I have today, the ones who taught me my normalcy, Jack and Jill first introduced me to nearly all of them.

Will Edwards is one of them; he's been a consistent character in the crew. The brotha is stretched-out like taffy, put-together and debonair, with an angled jaw that's most often locked shut. Upon first sight, he seems of the serious sort. Really, he's introverted—a trait easily misinterpreted, particularly in a Black body. Once past that guard, he's a dorky goof. Or a goofy dork. Every few months, from the social media abyss, surfaces a video of Will shimmying wildly to Britney Spears—dancing like no one was watching, to the delight of all who were. That's really all you need to know about Will.

He and I spent much of childhood on passing ships. Our families joined neighboring Jack and Jill chapters. We went to rival high schools. He attended Howard while I made my way through Georgetown. For years, our relationship didn't extend further than those Jack and Jill events—we'd exchange dap and bounce. But for us both, the organization proved to be just the introduction, a prelude of exposure to what token tables could be. Martha's Vineyard brought our worlds together.

The Mecca of all token tables floats off Cape Cod's coastline. To the uninducted, Martha's Vineyard conjures images of white wealth draped in salmon colors and cable-knit—the island's reputation is still built upon the Kennedy Onassis legacy. But

Blacks frequented her shores long before the first family laid claim. Records of our time on the island stretch to the 1700s, as enslaved people first. By the end of that century, Blacks had established a community in the Farm Neck neighborhood of the island. Throughout the 1800's we came as runaways, indentured servants, and whalers, then later as houseworkers. By the early twentieth century, Blacks were traveling in critical mass as escapees of another sort, seeking refuge from hot Harlem summers. The list of visitors to migrate to the island is an American history textbook: Frederick Douglass, Ethel Waters, Adam Clayton Powell, Madam C. J. Walker, Martin Luther King Jr., Dorothy West, and Vernon Jordan, to name a few. Today, as for over a hundred years, it is a haven. The East Coast's Black business people, doctors, athletes, entertainers, and President frolic alike.

Will painstakingly pieced together his Black identity in the pre-Vineyard days. He drew from what he could. He loved the *Fresh Prince of Bel-Air*—Will Smith was his favorite. Will's fashion, slang, and moves were morsels to devour, even if they were dated by the time the reruns reached home. BET was a treasure trove; *106 and Park* introduced the soundtrack he sought. Will made a small number of Black friends while young and harvested culture from them as well, mimicked their jaunt and drawl. Despite it all, the ambivalence only deepened. All showed him what he wasn't, but nothing showed him what he was. Or would be. *I was either too white for the Blacks or too Black for the whites.*

Martha's Vineyard provided him his first reference point. It gave him anchoring. From his initial voyage, Will encountered people who were unique in that they dubbed him ordinary. They opened Will's eyes to the array of options before him—options that had been obscured from view in his suburban bedroom. Options beyond those that existed on the TV screen. He saw some of himself in these people, and their likeness put him at ease. For the first time, Will felt comfortable peering inward and exploring what he unearthed, *cause no one's really trying to tell me I'm too white or too privileged or too Black.*

Will can pinpoint the moment he realized he'd found a home. It was a scene altogether mundane—kids ragging on each other in a park the same way they do in every corner of the world. They busted jokes at each other's expense and rolled to the ground when the punchlines hit. When they didn't, they laughed doubly hard. To him, it was euphoric. Will was sixteen and had never been so at ease. He looked around and thought, *I love this.*

It is on Martha's Vineyard that I, too, feel most myself. Most average. Day-to-day ruminations on Blackness, constantly calculating the role your precise level of Blackness plays in every interaction, wears you out. It's exhausting. The Vineyard is a space to exhale. A feeling of relief washes over me when her painted porches and buzzing beaches enter view. It is physically felt. It's like those final moments before slumber—pulse slowing to a lazy thud, muscles, once tightly wound, unraveling on their spools, and a breath containing the day's worries weaseling away through parted lips. The relief comes with knowledge that, for the coming days, I will be my whole self. The Vineyard is a home as Maya Angelou describes it should be: *The safe place where we can go as we are and not be questioned.* That is why we flock. That is the warm sensation we yearn for. Acceptance.

But, as with all things, these token tables are not without their own complexities. Sebastian and Will are best friends—their names are conjoined the way that Devon and mine are—but Bas does not paint quite so rosy a picture of the spaces where we find home.

Bas is bothered by the exclusivity he sees in token tables. He has no use for the hypocrisy we willfully blind ourselves to. He argues that these spaces are not only a retreat from the pressures of a white world, but an evasion of broader Black life: *A lot of the people in Jack and Jill or Martha's Vineyard can't interact with Black people who aren't really educated and affluent.* He sees elitism. He sees snobbishness. He sees contradictions. It is grievously inconsistent, he argues, for one to rush to isolation as a response to Black exclusion, and then make it one's business to exclude other Blacks from entering one's utopian fabrication.

The point is unoriginal, not in the sense that it is generic, but in the sense that it is time-honored. Charges of elitism were levied at Marion Turner Stubbs Thomas then, just as today they are laid at the feet of the litter of little ones who matriculate from her organization. Martha's Vineyard, to many, means bougie-this and bougie-that.

It's a valid point. But it's not the whole story.

By definition, of course, participation requires leapfrogging a financial barrier that is beyond the reach of many. Anyone with the time and money to *summer* anywhere is a shade of elite.

Nor is the potential elitism simply economic. An air of superiority can come with spending too much time in these alternate universes. *But for the grace of God go I*, gets lost out there. People *start to smell theyselves*, as my grandfather, Pop, would've said. We lose sight of our interconnectedness, retroactively stratifying our race by standards that were not of our own creation. Jack and Jill has a long history of colorism, no doubt. *Good hair* finds a home in greater numbers on the Vineyard than elsewhere, as does disdain for all things *ghetto*. A shared struggle in history did not fortify our people against those same forces that separate the posh from the proletariat in white society, attaching extensive value to arbitrary traits and very little to character.

I've witnessed instances of this elitist attitude coming to bear—discussions about what kind of people are allowed at *our* beach and *our* parties had in a way that pushed an inclusive pronoun to its most exclusive extent.

But I have also seen the horde of *say what?*s that swarm in to greet those comments. I've met the many people like Sebastian, who place greater value on pan-Blackness than all else. And they vastly outnumber the country-clubbing, caviar-consuming, self-denigrating Black folk who seldom, and most often mythologically, exist.

There is also a larger plus to counterbalance the acknowledged minuses. For people like me, Martha's Vineyard and Jack and Jill and all those other safe spaces ministering to us token kids served an indispensable role, bringing together wanderers who would have otherwise drifted through life untethered to a community. They provided affirmation that we are not alien.

Despite his criticisms, even Sebastian can pinpoint a moment of brilliance the Vineyard brought him. His is like Will's in both banality and profundity:

I remember looking around and seeing everyone just enjoying themselves outside. It was just a whole bunch of nice, young, African American kids just enjoying themselves carefree for however many hours. I acknowledged at that point that this was something extremely, extremely special. There was a moment where I was like, this is just an extremely special situation, and I tend to think that it's going to last a very long time.

How marvelous and saddening it is for a young man of his age to discover such wonder in belonging.

BAD, BAD, NOT GOOD

THE FIRST TIME I tried, one of the boys told me I did it wrong. I brought the bowl to my lips, let the smoke fill my cheeks, swished it around like I was gargling Listerine, and spat it back out, not yet brave enough to dispel it through my nostrils. The sour, earthy taste coated my mouth, but I curled my lips into a thin grin anyhow, then made a show of stumbling as though the THC had been injected into my brain. *Man . . .* he said. *You didn't even hit it. You have to inhale.* Fine. I tried again, this time sucking in deeply, setting the lit ember in the glass bowl aglow. *Now hold it . . . hold it . . . hold it . . .* I hacked my guts up. Breathing felt like pulling hot steam through a coffee stirrer. The older kids cackled so hard their eyes filled with tears.

In the timeline of my life, I fudge the details a bit and deem that night the start of puberty. I was an eleven-year-old fifth grader. Nearly two more years passed before I weighed over

100 pounds, three before my voice dropped, and, to this day, I await the beard I was promised. But that was the first harbinger of what was to come. The first of the transformations to trickle through. The ones that defined the early teenage years.

The trickle ratcheted up through sixth grade and, by seventh, it'd grown torrential. The kids I knew gravitated to grown-up stuff and I submerged myself to my chin. Weed became a guiding force. Many kids had tunnel vision for it: who was selling; who was buying; who was smoking and how. You would've thought it was crack the way so many obsessed, acting out rap lyric fantasies of serving and getting served. It was the great democratizer, giving young kids a reason to talk to old, and boys to girls. It also formalized a new pecking order. One's proximity to weed, familiarity with the associated lingo and customs, indicated "cool." It wouldn't be long before the coolest of those cool kids would swim into increasingly illicit waters. Several would hit rehab before graduation—a decidedly uncool place to land. But their early experimental phases mimed a maturity we all mimicked.

Sex creeped into the collective conscious at the same time and for the same reason as weed. Danger was the zeitgeist. We all searched for ways to appear as something other than precisely what we were—powerless, confused, and uncertain. The shirts and skorts over at the girls' school became skimpier, complemented by Uggs and heavy eyeliner. It was a look. The boys grew more boisterous, inflating ourselves to fill more space.

Sex, the act, hadn't yet arrived for most. Sex, the deity, reigned forcibly—omnipresent and persuasive.

Race completed this new, unholy trinity. Like weed and sex, it competed with innocence to lay claim to us all. And like weed and sex, it made its presence known in loud ways. White kids learned the word "nigga" and threw it between themselves through giggles for sport. White kids saw candidate Barack Obama and parroted the racist punchlines they found on Facebook. White kids watched their first music videos and confused those fantasies for reality. Insisted I was too Black. Insisted I wasn't Black enough.

But race crept in with more maniacal nuance as well.

I'd known Ben, my best friend at the time, since kindergarten. We both had working moms, and we forged our friendship on weekday evenings long after the other kids had been picked up from school. Ben and I were a pair. We knew it and so did the world. But Ben was white,[9] and suddenly the world relabeled me Ben's best *Black* friend, as if demoting the affection I felt to the minor leagues.

I remember the prevailing feeling of ugliness that darkened that era. I felt, above all else, ugly. In part, due to subtleties in language and deed, like the added adjective between "best" and "friend." The sheepish way my invitations evaporated for events where boys and girls paired off. A standard of beauty so strictly defined—swooping, blonde locks for the boys that could be

---

9   At time of writing, Ben and I are still besties and Ben is still white.

flipped at will. Messaging that my (admittedly gangly) features were unfit. Suspicion that my skin was most problematic of all.

But also, in part because, well, not infrequently, girls called me ugly.

I felt rejected from this rebellious revolution that surrounded me, though I fought for my place within it. I could see the epicenter from my perch but tumbled and flailed anytime I drew near. We were all negotiating the wave of newness, but race, my being a token, magnified those natural teenage discomforts and presented new ones as well. It ensured that my difference, my isolation, was not merely hormonal, conceptual or internal. My difference could be perceived and pointed to. Defined even. My DNA was the problem. My otherness was fact-based. Scientific.

It dragged me to a confused place. It left me unmoored.

One evening in the spring of seventh grade, I collapsed onto the floor of my bedroom, head rolled back onto my duvet, choking up salty tears and snot. Mama and Faith were out shopping, Dad was gone as well, so I was left to wallow freely. Cutting was in vogue among the troubled sort in those days. I gave it a shot, and it wasn't for me. I dreaded pain but welcomed what the act represented—the possibility of an end.

Teary-eyed, I scanned the bedroom. I rolled my eyes over the second-story windows, jars of chemical ointments and creams, a serrated knife from last night's dinner—other possibilities. On my desk sat a yo-yo—a wooden, vintage-looking model from Cracker Barrel or the Colonial Williamsburg gift shop. The trinket reemerged from the bowels of my room every so often; it was not well-designed. The string was so impractically long that the best one could hope for was to drag the spool, fancifully walking a stubborn dog. I glanced at the toy then returned to my resting state, staring at the ceiling fan above. I looked back to the toy. Then the fan again. A plan formed.

Inhale. I rose from the hardwood. I'd been sitting long enough that my butt deadened, so my first step dropped with a shaky limp. Exhale. I crossed the room to the desk, grabbed the yo-yo and chair, and carried both into the spotlight just below the fan. Inhale. I placed my right foot onto the chair, then my left, and tied the toy, bulb side up, to the fan. I watched the string fall, the finger hole at the bottom creating a tiny, action figure–size fitted noose. Exhale. I looped the long string around my neck once, then again. An Uncle had given me a wilderness manual a few years prior (only God knows why) and I flipped through it occasionally. There was a whole chapter on knots. *How hard can it be?* Inhale. I tied the string like shoelaces, then knotted the loops again, and again, and again, until there was nothing left to hold.

Exhaaaaaaaaaale. My arms drifted back to my sides. I'd stopped sobbing by then. Nothing to do now but drop and stare. I stared at the blank wall ahead until my vision blurred. A decade passed. I inched my big toes off the edge. Another decade, and my middle toes followed. Now for the pinky. I waited, gathered my resolve.

There's something fittingly juvenile about my logic here.

Likely neither twine nor fan would have supported even my pre-growth-spurt frame. But it's the thought that counts, and I had a mind for mortality.

Sliding forward, a breath from eternity. The front door squealed open and commotion blew in with it. Faith and Ma never returned from their day-long escapades in a neutral state—ecstasy or agony, no half-stepping. Which was it today? Their arrival added urgency to the matter at hand. Either climb down right this instant or step off the chair and into oblivion. For the first time, I imagined Ma calling me to dinner, then sending Faith up to retrieve me. For the first time I imagined what she'd find, what it would do to her.

All forms of self-destruction are selfish, the premeditated variety most of all. I climbed down.

In the timeline of my life, this too is a marker. A beginning, rather than an end. Things had to worsen before I found my way out of the forest.

Over the next eighteen months, change was the only constant. The weed-craze caught up with me. I found trouble and my parents brought their wrath down hard. My grandfather fell ill. My parents split. My father left home. High school arrived.

Beneath it all, my teenage turmoil rolled on.

Early winter of ninth grade, I awoke one Saturday in earth-shaking pain. I'd gotten migraines occasionally, but this was explosive. It struck first behind the eyes, pulsing through each vein. Then it seeped like a slow-moving oil spill, inching to new territory and blackening it. I tossed in darkness for hours, unable to bear volume above a whisper. All through the morning hours I waited out the siege. By lunchtime, I thought I might vomit. I'd resisted medication on the principle of macho austerity, but when afternoon came, I was desperate for relief.

I toppled down to the kitchen through fog. The drawer under the microwave contained the miscellaneous: crayons, school pictures of distant cousins, strangers' business cards, the leveler, poignant fortune cookie prophecies. I reached for the Excedrin Migraine bottle and shook it: plenty left. *Under 18: Consult a physician.* Okay, fifteen, but old for my age. *Over 18: Max 2 per day.* Two it is. I sucked my cheeks for saliva then threw both down the gullet and swallowed them dry, action movie style.

I zombied to the TV room and Titanic'd to the couch. I flicked on *MTV Jams*, but I promptly muted it and shut my eyes to the flashes. The stiff knocking behind my eyelids continued. Fifteen minutes passed and the pills had yet to dull the gnawing in my head. I felt it all over now. Enough. I squinted and dragged back to the utility drawer for two more, then I returned to my spot on the couch. I bellyached and floundered longer. It wrested my senses. Five Lil Wayne features went by and the pain had yet to subside. I visited the drawer again.

Between the third and fourth cycle, the throbbing quieted, but another pain inched its way forward. A familiar foe. This was first semester of my freshman year. The Lax Bros had just, consciously or otherwise, evicted me; the Black Table had yet to adopt me. I felt a waif. I'd known since I woke that morning that the migraine was temporary. At fifteen, with precious little perspective to hold, the isolation seemed endless. I had had enough. I returned to the drawer and finished the bottle.

My mind made up, there was no turning back. Excedrin would not be enough. I recalled the small bottle of leftover prescription meds collecting dust on my bedroom window sill. A fight a few months prior had sent me to the hospital for a night and home with a dozen or so white tablets.[10] They weren't very potent but there was, I assumed, strength in numbers. Just as with the Excedrin bottle, I soon found the bottom.

Old-school joints played in the living room when I got back, but I didn't focus for long. The effects crashed in waves. My eyes betrayed me, turning my vision doubled and duplicitous. The videos on the screen stretched, fuzzed, and starkened like fauvist paintings. The couch turned to a raft in tumultuous seas. A pit of nausea fixed itself in my stomach. I gripped the cushions for dear life as the room rocked.

Staying afloat is exhausting. Vertigo gave way to fatigue. I tossed, but my movements came in rusty, mechanical juts, delayed and decelerated. Soon after, I felt nothing—not the nausea and certainly not the lonesomeness. I was numb and tired, my

---

10 Fight is generous. It was a tap dance. I traveled to a neighborhood I shouldn't have and became inducted upon arrival. Once they'd surrounded me, somebody's big brother stepped into the circle. He offered a low-toned apology before our collision. I understood. The hand had to be played as it'd been dealt. He struck first, then mounted my back. I collapsed to the pavement, overwhelmed. Then his posse joined in. They fractured ego and bone. Philly is a big, small town. By the end of the school day Monday, I'd known who was responsible. A family friend pushed us to press charges. Serious charges. I said no thanks. He and I were interchangeable. The hand had to be played as it'd been dealt.

eyes droopy, and my spirit waterlogged. The lids closed themselves, and I sunk into a suffocating slumber.

When I shivered awake on the couch the following afternoon, I greeted a world of confusion. My clothes were damp with sweat and my entire body ached. I didn't know why. Once the explanation dawned on me, so too did disappointment. But also, a small measure of relief. I told no one about the failed attempt, moved on as though unphased, and did my best to put the hazy evening out of mind. The problems didn't disappear, but as days and weeks wore on, it became apparent that death would not be the simple solution I hoped for. I'd have to find a more sustainable fix.

Today, my remembrances of the not-as-good times are steeped in shame. Adults tend to regard the hardships of a thirteen-year-old private school kid in strictly patronizing terms, even if that kid was you. Perhaps especially if that kid was you.

Nearly a decade now separates me from the last of those encounters with finality, if you can even call them that, but the emotions of the time, the smallness, still feel close. So too does the isolation: feeling apart from the world while childhood uncertainty transformed to adult anxiety.

But you were a teenager!

The peanut gallery chimes,

We all felt alone!

Granted. Growing up is a grotesque process and the terror only differs in degree.

But kids cope with chaos by rushing the familiar. We form

ingroups (and outgroups) for safety's sake. It's natural but doesn't bode well for the greyboys and greygirls among us who have little security to turn to. So yes, I am sure much of what I felt was normal teenage stuff, but much of it wasn't. Much of it was the compounding effect of dissimilarity. How much exactly? I'll never know.

Despite my best efforts, I lived to see tenth grade, thanks in large part to my own ineptitude. But ineptitude would not see me through the times to come. To make it much further, I'd need to process through that heaping pile of ambivalence that delivered me to the brink. I'd need to construct an identity that could withstand ever-shifting sands. My brothers at the Black Table were the first and most necessary lifeline. They ushered me a long way on that journey to Self. But they weren't alone. The identity I claimed was rooted in something much deeper than they could provide. Only in retrospect has that grounding become clear.

Hey Mama

—Kanye West

Love, Mom

Dear Cole,

Son, there are certain pivotal seasons in one's childhood that shape the person one becomes. I did not see yours for what it was until after it was too late to soften the blow. Your most tumultuous period came early in your young life.

I should have seen you building up to it throughout seventh grade. You made new friends—kids who had too much freedom, too much money, and too few guardrails. I overheard your conversations with them change with each passing week from usual boyish mischief, to girls and stories about who-did-what and how-they-got-away-with-it. I chalked it up to puberty. As the school year rolled on, your disposition changed from excited, easygoing, and curious to quiet, distant, and uninterested. You were not happy. I feared that you were flying too close to the sun and, unlike your white friends, the consequences of doing so could be irreparable. I am deeply sorry that we missed the minor signs for months, until they became unavoidable.

We visited Ethiopia the following Easter. Your grandparents doted on Faith, since it was her first trip, leaving you and me some time to talk. We had our first long conversation in a while and the emotional toll of your year of trials became apparent. You were miserable inside and had been keeping it a secret for months. You hadn't processed all that happened that year as well as it appeared, and you were confused by the tension at home. I was first stunned, but then I experienced a range of emotions. The one I remember most was the deep mourning over the loss of your innocence at such a young age. I was also angry—mostly with myself. I failed to help you brace for the impact. Even today, I can't read about it without tears and deep regret. I thank God that he stepped in where I failed, guiding us all to a better place.

You sent your manuscript to me with a request that I reflect on my own pivotal years, the brief span of time when I took my greatest strides from childhood to womanhood like the trials you experienced between those two difficult summers. I've done so reluctantly because there's far too much to say in one letter. Pivotal moments happen repeatedly, with each one setting the foundation for those to come. In order to understand my early transition, you'd have to know better the world I grew up in.

You have heard me reference my complicated childhood. When people ask me basic questions like, "How many siblings do you have?" or, "Where are you from?" you have heard my rehearsed response: "That's a quick question but a very long answer." And so, it is a long story.

Your Grandma Marta gave birth to me in Albuquerque, New Mexico, shortly before she graduated from college in the US. Soon after I was born, Grandma Marta returned to her native Ethiopia, leaving me in what she thought were better arms. For most of my childhood, I was reared by Grandma Hattie, who you never knew, and Charles Roberts. I can't tell you much about Albuquerque; the three of us moved to Germany before I entered kindergarten. Charles became one of the few Negro men serving on a small Air Force base in Birkenfeld. If he had been a single man, he would have lived in the barracks with the other single soldiers. But he was married, and someone in the hierarchy felt uncomfortable with Negro and white families cohabitating on military grounds—so uncomfortable that the military paid our expenses to live elsewhere.

If Hattie felt dismayed by the inherent bigotry in our forced move, the feeling was offset by her excitement to have a more genuinely German experience. She chose a quaint attic apartment in the home of yet another family you often heard of but never knew: the Beckers. The space suited us—it was charming and clean and the Beckers were a lovely couple with a son my age and, later, a baby girl. The boy, your "Uncle" Hans Herbert, was shorter than me with red hair and freckles. He was teased for being a ginger more often than I was teased for my dark skin. I felt sorry for him and remember thinking that my skin color was more explainable, since my parents were brown, and everyone seemed to want to look like me. Girls always laid out to tan on sunny days. But no one liked his blotchy freckles. No one except me.

I attended an international boarding school nearby with girls from all over the world and I thought nothing of our differences. That was my normal. In second grade we learned about Hitler and the plight of Jews. I remember feeling sad for them and thankful Hattie hadn't endured such misery when she was young. School never taught us about the struggles colored folks faced, but Hattie ensured I knew the basics. The granddaughter of a slave, Hattie talked about the injustices of slavery and Jim Crow. I knew people were still struggling to achieve civil rights in the US. I remember the grief and sadness the adults expressed when the Kennedys and Martin Luther King were assassinated. But the life I knew in Germany seemed far removed from that world. I didn't yet fully understand the direct impact prejudice could have on me.

We went to base sometimes on weekends for Hattie's bowling league. She expressed her "gratitude" loud and proud when we encountered the officers who enforced the racist housing rule. She made it clear that separating us was their loss, not ours. She called it "the silver lining in a cloud of stupidity," as she preferred experiencing Germany with Germans, rather than living with Americans who reconstructed their segregated US lifestyle on that base. By imploring them to keep the rule, she reminded them of its racist motivation.

Hattie loved her heritage and wore her identity well. She

bragged to our German neighbors about the beauty of her culture—the art, books, music, and Southern food. They looked
forward to the rare occasions when she and the Beckers had
everyone over for parties. Motown played as she made gumbo
and bragged about Baldwin and Aretha. Neighbors arrived early, hungry, and in numbers, then went home late—well-fed and
carrying a borrowed album or book.

Hattie's second love was antiques. She became a dealer while
in Europe and developed a keen eye for parsing reproductions
from originals. When visiting the little shops and estate sales
nearby, she sometimes found herself in the company of Germans who were not so open to her differences. Hattie used to
say to me that "one of the best things about bigots is that they
will often underestimate you, which gives you the upper hand."
She spotted them instinctively, just as she did reproductions.
She said that racist Germans behaved much like bigots in the
American South. So, she wasn't intimidated when she sensed
their racist attitudes. She smiled and leaned into it, as if she
enjoyed the sport of it.

I remember when, on one visit to an antique market, a shopkeeper we met refused to shake her outstretched hand. Unbothered, she perused his shop and politely suggested that one of his
chairs was tagged incorrectly. He brushed off her suggestion
dismissively. Instead of showing indignance, Hattie turned her
polite smile into a grin and exaggerated her southern drawl, almost singing her response: "Yassuh, I only have an eighth grade
education but learned 'bout French anteeks from TV shows in

Loosana, when I was a nappy little thing and from cleaning white folks' mancheens!" Her accent and the cleaning lie told me something was up, but the shopkeeper missed the cue. In his mind, she had only confirmed the prejudices he held, so he turned his attention to other shoppers. Hattie spent the next hour sizing up his wares and patiently waiting for all of the other buyers to finish striking their deals. Finally, there was just the shopkeeper and Hattie left—and a whole lot of unbought furniture that she knew he didn't want to take home.

What followed was a thing of beauty. She peppered him with amateurish questions, feeding his superiority complex. When their negotiations were over, the bigot returned home feeling triumphant—he thought he had finally unloaded several left-over fakes for a few dollars. Hattie went home with an authentic set of seventeenth century chairs and a desk worth more than the rest of his whole inventory. Over dinner that night, Hattie laughed while recounting the day's events to Charles and the Beckers: "You can't change a bigot," she said, "but you can make sure he pays for it!"

When I was nine years old, we visited the US for the first time in five years. Our flight landed in New York and we rented a car to drive to Charles's family in Kentucky and Ohio, before heading south to see Hattie's people. Each restaurant and rest stop along the way brought me into contact with a greater number of people that looked like me than I'd seen in my whole life up to that point. The relatives we visited all wore similar hairstyles, liked similar music, watched similar television shows and dressed in similar clothes—few of which were familiar to me. Unlike my circle of international friends in Germany, my relatives were all similar in ways that made me stand out. I was used to being different in Germany, a foreign country where everyone I knew was unique. Here I was "home," yet, for the first time, confronting the cultural elements of America's racial divide. Afros, hot pants, bell bottoms, and *Soul Train*—is this what it meant to be Black? I was perplexed.

I will always remember one brief stop we made on our road trip. We pulled over to a gas station and, while Charles pumped the gas, I scurried off to the bathroom. I'd made it halfway there when I felt a huge arm lift me by my waist and throw me back onto the pavement. I laid on the ground, hurt and shocked, looking up at the brawny white man who'd sent me tumbling. He pointed and yelled, "Go 'round back!" I picked myself up, rationalized that this was my punishment for trying to enter without wearing shoes, and headed toward the back door. As I cornered the building and looked up, I saw three doors labelled White Women, White Men, and Colored.

Hattie had told me that we had a relative nearby whose last name was White. She often bragged that he was a big deal in this part of Louisiana. Here was proof—two bathrooms just for his family! Well, I thought, since we were relatives, it was okay for me to use the White Women's room. And I did. Perhaps luckily, there was nobody inside.

When I returned to the car, I explained the scrapes on my knees and elbows to Hattie and Charles. I told them I'd found our family's bathroom. Charles turned to Hattie, "I told you! You had better talk to that girl of yours." Hattie sighed. Over the next several hours, they taught me the rules of behavior for colored folk in the American South.

My pivotal period began in summer just as yours did. From that conversation, through the rest of our visit, I confronted the bigotry that Hattie had left in the South. Perhaps if I'd grown up in the US, I would've just taken those events for granted. But having grown up in another world, in another life, the impact was so much stronger. Suddenly, the world in which I was so carelessly confident looked very different to me. By autumn, I understood. Over the next ten years, she and I often revisited that conversation and the other events of that trip. We called it my Summer of Truth.

Some of what happened in the years that followed should be familiar to you. We moved from Germany to Richmond, California. I stepped awkwardly into Black America. I tried and failed at both growing a 'fro and softening my accent. When I bumped into Huey Newton at a candy store near the Black Panthers' headquarters around the corner from our home, he thought I was a weird little girl with a big forehead. He was correct.

The high school years in California brought me more tumultuous times. Grandma Hattie lost her sight and left to attend a school for the blind. I moved into the home of our close friends, the Benfords. It was there, experiencing their loving, made-for-TV life, that I began to find my way. One of the children, Gail, became my closest confidant. She looked up to me, and for the first time, made me feel as though I belonged.

I took a job lifeguarding at the local YMCA to earn spending money. My new boss, Ada Cole, your namesake, provided the direction that I was missing. She had a magnetic presence, almost an aura, with substance at her core. She embodied what I, as a young girl in Germany, had hoped for my own future. She and your Aunt Gail provided a kind of acceptance, similar to your Black Table. That acceptance gave me the confidence to grow into my own version of me.

We lost Grandma Hattie when I was a college sophomore. Complications from diabetes—the same disease that claimed her sight—led to her death. Even though she had been in and out of the hospital for months, the loss was impossible to process. I was devastated. A year or so later, I was reunited with my birth family, who came to the US as political refugees. You and I have never really spoken of what that time was like for me, the swell of emotions that came from first losing Grandma Hattie and then meeting Grandma Marta. I'm sure that one day we will.

Your Ethiopian uncles and I quickly fell into our sibling roles, as if we had lived our whole lives together. I grew close to them, entering a new phase of my own life. This part you know well. You have spent time in Libet—our house in Indiana that Grandma Marta ruled over benevolently. You know the family she and Grandpa reared there—my brothers, plus first and extended cousins—fifty-nine kids in all! They told you of the time we spent treating it as the barracks, boys sleeping in one large room, girls sharing the bedrooms. They were naive to the realities of race in America. I spent many evenings explaining.

Years passed, your dad and I were married, and you were born in Indiana. Then your sister. Family members who lived in Libet and around Fort Wayne dispersed to every corner of the globe. The four of us were among the first to go. We moved to Philadelphia.

While you were still a toddler, I visited Yetebon, the Ethiopian village where your grandmother's family is from and where her organization, Project Mercy, built a school. One day, I met Grandma in the kitchen where she leaned over enormous pots of steaming vegetable soup that would become lunch for the 1,700 students. She turned away to introduce me to one of the village elders, a very distinguished old man who had come, not just for lunch, but to do his special work. She explained to me that, like his father, grandfather, and generations of men before them, this man was gifted with the ability to remember the family trees of everyone who descended from this area. After lunch we sat on a porch overlooking a massive oak tree and the man recited our ancestry:

Hajl Ibrahim Yahmedel Bedwi begat
Kenema Hajl Ibrahim, who begat
Dukema Kenema, who begat
Wudimo Dukema, who begat
Ahbo Wudimo, who begat
Tayo Ahbo, who begat
Yarbo Tayo, who begat

Badgegrad Yarbo, who begat

Yazma Mendel Badgegrad, who begat

Garro Yazma Mendel, who begat

Remsiso Garro, who begat

Aliye Remsiso, who begat

Gabre-Tsadick Aliye, who begat

Marta Gabre-Tsadick, your grandmother, who begat

Yemisrach Bereket Demeke (a.k.a. Mama, to you), who begat

Cole Thomas Demeke Brown, and your sister, Faith Desta
Brown

Such a long list, representing centuries! Could this be true?
I was skeptical at first, so I asked him to recite the names over
again and again. He repeated the series of names from memory,
in identical succession, until I had carefully documented each
one. He hesitated only when he got to the new ones—mine,
yours, and Faith's—pronouncing the Western parts slowly to
be sure he had them right.

Then he expanded beyond names and shared what he knew
about many of the ancestors. He spoke with such granularity,
placing importance on each person's life. Kenema was a strong
fighter; Ahbo, a tradesman; several were elders and leaders of
villages. He pointed to one of the women who lived on the com-
pound, then spoke of the brother of Garro and named his de-
scendants in order to explain why she was my fourth cousin
once removed. After that, he wanted to hear our names again

and questioned me about our lives in America. I'm sure he added our stories to the library in his mind.

Your family's roots can be traced back through many generations in the place where civilization began. I missed knowing this heritage as a child. That's why, when I became a mother, I was so determined to prepare you and Faith for this American life, but also to make certain you knew there was a broader definition of African American, just as valid, and just as available to you.

Even today, you must remember one of the conversations I made you and your sister suffer through over and over again.

Me: Who are you, and what does that mean?

You: Oh no, not again, Mom.

Me: C'mon, it's not hard. Repeat after me, "We are the proud children and the legacy and the pride of our ancestors who changed the world."

You: We . . . are the proud children and . . . the legacy and the pride of our ancestors who . . . changed the world.

Me: Yes, but what does that *mean*?

You: It means we must be the best we can be!

Your dad and I feared that you would grow physically before you really understood those words. His parents were both civil rights champions and Grandma Helen taught her son early. "Black people in America don't get the luxury of making mistakes, so be careful," were the words we passed on to you and your sister.

I envisioned scenes of you undergoing a growth spurt that left you looking older than your years. You'd walk down the street and notice a woman clutching her purse or crossing to the other side to avoid you—someone who would be blind to your humanity. What would that do to your confidence and sense of self? And, since your emotions were often so opaque, how would I know it had affected you badly? What other dangers could come from it? Since our people arrived on these shores, every generation of African Americans has faced the terror of young men wrongfully murdered. None was more personal to me than when I spoke with Ron Davis after his son, Jordan, was tragically murdered in Jacksonville. Young, beautiful Jordan was your age.

The realities of racism and hatred were lurking, and the danger felt real. I prayed long and hard that you would win this battle for your dignity without sacrificing your safety. I could see the signs, even when you were still a child, and even in our so-called enlightened world. We rehearsed those words because I wanted them to roll off your tongue so naturally that whenever someone suggested you were not as good as those around you, the phrase would resurface in your mind.

The pivotal season of your life did come, as I knew it would, and you were tested for months on end. Yes, there are defining periods in one's life. They change one forever. But if you are tuned in, you get to choose how. I am so immensely proud of you, a man who grew out of his own summer of truth to become self-aware and thoughtful, one whose faith and character steer him to the right decisions when it matters most.

Love,
Mom

Parents Understand

I CLOSED MY EYES tight, held my breath, and braced myself. The anxiety struck hard as I choked out my final words of pleading. Too late! The belt came down heavy. I jumped as it made impact and guided my hands to the crash site to assess the damage. The good news was my backside was still very much intact; the bad news was that Pop was already in motion, winding up for another round. I kept my hands there as long as possible but moved them on his command. Another cycle of groans, grunts, and grimaces began as Pop proceeded to whip my butt.

Butt whippings were a regular occurrence in my younger days. My seventy-six-year-old Pop was oftentimes on the other end of them. When he needed help keeping me in line, he called upon Leroy and Oscar for backup.

Leroy and Oscar. The gruesome twosome. Just the mention of either name struck fear into my heart as a child. My Pops handpicked both tools and could conduct a full symphony with either. Leroy was a fly swatter. I have to commend my Pops on creativity there. I've been hit by a lot of people with a lot of things in my life, but no one (save for Pop) ever thought to reach for the fly swatter. Pop had a special wrist technique that, when done properly, could make Leroy sting to no end. Imagine a whole colony of bees eating at your backside simultaneously. He would chase me all around the house screaming, "Boy! Get down here and meet Leroy." I had no choice but to oblige. I was introduced and reintroduced to Leroy several times between the ages of three and eleven. He was never friendly.

Oscar was my nemesis. Meet with Oscar once and you wouldn't be able to sit down for a week. He was an old, cracked, leather belt with a big gold buckle that my Pops had worn for a hundred years, at least. Oscar gave Pop that portability factor that one looks for in a good spanking device. Pop couldn't always show up to places with a fly swatter in hand, but he always wore a belt. Oscar made it possible for Pop to whip my butt in a whole host of situations that would be otherwise unachievable: at the grocery store, in fancy restaurants. More than once, he pulled it off while driving—slowed the car to an inching roll along the highway, reached back with his right hand while maintaining his grip of the steering wheel with the left, and swatted at me without ever taking his eyes off the road.

I remember the day Oscar finally broke in half after years of heinie hitting. He split right across the middle leaving nothing left to swing with. In a truly "Pop" manner, my grandfather stopped the beating, left the room, and came back five minutes later with Oscar in one hand and a roll of duct tape in the other. Oscar and his shiny silver cast then finished the job he had started.

Believe it or not, these are some of my fondest memories. The summers I spent with Pop were never easy—most of my time was used begging my parents to come get me—but it was in this time that I learned what it is to be a man. He was always rough on me, demanded my best, but even in the midst of all this aggression I never doubted his love for me. I owe everything I am to him. The Pop I grew up with is all but gone now; the dementia took him from me, but I will always remember the time we spent together. I would give anything in the world to spend just one more summer down in Fort Wayne, Indiana with Leroy, Oscar, and Pop.

———

I wrote those words as a tenth grader at Penn Charter in response to an essay prompt my English teacher, Dr. Harris, had assigned the class. Dr. Harris was *Doctor* Harris, and she corrected those who called her anything else. She was accomplished and self-impressed and flirtatious. And white. At the time of the assignment, my paternal grandfather drifted in a strange purgatorial state between life and death. Following a dementia diagnosis and a string of strokes, his mind and identifying personality traits had all but evaporated, leaving behind a relatively healthy, yet empty, shell. Pop and I were close, but I recognized from a young age that he was, as grandfathers often are, the product of a different time.

Pop was of a bygone era of Black man in this country that people of all generations are right to remember as *the good ol' days*. Pop's daddy barely dodged slavery and his son was a Fortune 100 executive—his generation turned the corner. Even in his most feeble state, Pop could still tell you that he was on his way to church when the bombs eviscerated Pearl Harbor, regretfully a few years too young to join the fight, but the decades that followed carried plenty of struggle for him to imbibe. By the time I was born in 1995, Pop had fought through a war (Korea), an epidemic (crack), and a movement (duh), not to mention burying two parents, one wife, and sixteen, yes sixteen, full-blooded siblings. The struggle became him. He carried it in his body. It carved deep ridges across his forehead and down into his cheeks. Struggle was the life fluid that filled him, and it was struggle that secreted from his pores when exertion dampened his brow. So yes, Pop was tough, but so was the world. His disposition had been earned, not predestined.

And that is not to say he wasn't caring. Pop's warmth was of a vintage all his own. It was during those Indiana summers that we watched fuzzy John Wayne movies together on VHS, gorging feasts of Vienna Sausages and Fig Newtons. I was in tow on his trips to the American Legion, sipping cranberry juice while he sucked on his corn-husk pipe and reminisced with the other fixtures. He taught me how to play solitaire and showed me how he turned grapes to wine in his basement for the whole neighborhood to enjoy. I knew that he loved me like nobody's business; it was clear as day in his strut as we trounced around town, and I reaped immeasurable delight from producing such pride. The many endearing, rough-around-the-edges traits had sunk to his deepest recesses by the time Dr. Harris handed me that assignment sheet, and I wrote the essay to commemorate Pop's fleeting vigor. Disease had stolen his presence; the thought of losing our memories was too much to bear.

I labored to capture the romantic nostalgia I felt for my lost-in-time grandfather and our Midwestern summers, and when all was said and done, I felt I had done just that. To me, there is something inherently hilarious about an ornery, old man naming a flyswatter so that he can inconspicuously pull a six-year-old child in line around white folk.

Dr. Harris missed the punchline. Soon after I'd handed the paper in, I received an email in my inbox in which she described her visceral reaction. She was horrified at my abuse, empathetic to my suffering, and reverential of my vulnerability. She attached an article written by former NBA star, Jerry West, where he described in great detail the violence he endured throughout his own childhood. *Your story reminded me of his*, she said, presumably so that I'd appreciate that greatness could be born of abusive beginnings.

Her reaction was so ridiculous as to be almost comical. I told her so. Dr. Harris caught me in a delicate time—the memories of Pop's heyday had been written and all but shelved—an unideal moment to challenge the goodness of his legacy. We met—first just the two of us, then the head of upper school joined. Then, a fate we all hoped to avoid: my parents got involved.

Mama stormed to the school steps and raised hell. My father called in and tag-teamed the battle. *How dare she. . . .* They both thought her fears to be ingenuine (she had not, after all, called my abuse to the attention of her superiors or the authorities).

When it was my father's turn to chime in, he didn't mince words—I don't remember if he actually called her a racist, but I know he came mighty close. The whole fiasco was ultimately blown far out of proportion, included a brief cameo from the Reverend Al Sharpton, and made for a very awkward second semester of tenth grade English.[11]

Fast-forward three years and I was rounding out the first semester of my freshman year at Georgetown when I received a melancholic call from Mama. Pop's years-long struggle had entered its final act. I left for home the next morning, and I drove straight to the hospital when I arrived. We snapped our last pictures; I said my last *I love you.* And to my surprise, he left me with a gift: mumbled, *I love you too* for the first time in years. He grimaced through a toothy, oblivious smile as I slipped out of the room. He died the following morning.

Pop's service would be held the following week and I would offer the eulogy. Faith and I were his only grandchildren, and I was much closer to him than she. Our relationship made me the most logical choice. I accepted the responsibility when asked, as was my duty, but in truth, it petrified me. What to say of a man who had imparted so much in the way of history and spine?

In desperation I remembered that essay I'd written about Oscar, Leroy, and Pop only a few years prior. I dismantled my

11 Early in the dispute, I threatened to phone civil rights leaders and picket the school—another joke that Dr. Harris took seriously. That part she did report to her superiors. One afternoon, weeks after things had blown over, I had a new voicemail waiting . . . from the Reverend Al Sharpton. *Glad you set things straight, Cole. I was preparing to march.* He turned a once funny punchline downright hilarious.

room in search of it, finally digging it up from the depths of my desk drawers. Dr. Harris's comments were still attached, and I smirked recalling the then-dramatic ordeal that seemed so trivial in hindsight. I folded the paper up and stuffed it into the inside pocket of my best suit.

The day of the service, the pastor closed out his comments with somber optimism before introducing me to the overflowing congregation. With my eyes, I willed him to slow his walk from the podium. To turn around and announce we'd be skipping my speech instead. Ma squeezed my thigh on cue. I scanned the scribbled writing across my pages, hearing the phrases in Dr. Harris's voice, suddenly fearful that this group too would miss the joke. I rose from the church's front pew and strode to the lectern in mechanically measured strides. I spread the crumpled papers across the lectern, poorly tightening the wrinkles and flattening the creases. I cleared my throat once, twice, three times and fingered the double-staple fastened to the corner of the page. I tried to ignore Dr. Harris's comments. Finally, I began.

At first there was silence, but when I introduced the crowd to Leroy, I caught Aunt Sput's chuckle from the pews. Cousin Chloe imagined Pop hooking to slap while driving and lightened, allowing the warm, bitter tears to track down her cheeks and chap her lips. The whole room erupted in a chorus of laughter when Pop duct-taped his belt mid-swing. Even my father in the front row grinned, remembering his own tough Midwestern summers. I scanned from the podium to see relief and a wave of bobbing heads. In the end, the crowd loved it.

The congregation of that Baptist church understood what Dr. Harris couldn't: as Black kids, we are just parented differently.

Those differences amounted in ways large, small, and inconsistent. I am not one to now suggest, after all this talk, that Black parents are a monolith. But speak to enough kids, and trends appear. For tokens, our surroundings only magnified the uniqueness of that upbringing. The myriad differences were independently trivial, but when combined, they marked a drastic departure from the white norm that surrounded us.

Veronica Graves, a fellow Martha's Vineyard, Jack and Jill token, pointed out the first of these differences to me: *All my white friends called our friends' parents by their first names. I was raised to address people by Mr., and Mrs., and Ma'am, and Sir.* At twenty-two, she remembers the first time, nearly a decade prior, that a friend corrected her formal address, telling Veronica she could call her mother by her first name. Veronica nodded in agreement and scurried home that evening to report, *Mom, Lauren told me I could call her mom Karen from now on.* Veronica's mother responded the same way mine had countless times under similar circumstances, *Absolutely not. I don't care what Lauren said. I don't care what her mother said. You will address her as Mrs. So-and-so. A child does not call an adult by her first name. Period.*

Even now, as a bona fide working adult, Veronica still gets a creepy-crawly feeling each time friends' parents tell her to use their first names. She hears her mother's stern admonition, reminding her what is not appropriate.

I share her shivers. I remember the immediate regret of mistakenly calling Mrs. Grasso, "Marnie" or Mrs. Farley, "Nina" in my parents' presence. I remember the searing glares that closely followed. They spared me the public embarrassment, but delaying my comeuppance only prolonged the agony. All I could do was face forward, avoid eye contact, and pray they'd forget the misstep by the time we arrived home. They never did.

In our household, respect was not some abstract principle to be discussed and interpreted. Respect was learning to color inside the lines. Respect came with an instruction manual and play calling—traditional methods that time had scrubbed away from most of my peers. I can't count the number of times, in childhood, I stepped halfway through an entryway only to feel a vice grip on the scruff of my neck yanking me backward. A syrupy sweet voice overhead encouraging, *Please ma'am, after you.* I felt that same grip at times when I traipsed the inside lane while strolling through the city with Ma and Faith—the street-side is where I belonged. And there it was again when an elderly person entered view, *boy, you better git your ass up and go help that man.*

But on the hierarchy of home-training commandments, word was even greater than deed. Forgetting who you were talking to was a cardinal sin. Let a smidge of frustration seep into your speech when addressing adult figures and, if you were lucky, you'd get a *watch your tone, boy.* A touch too much 'tude? Or you caught the parents on a bad day? That was a pop in the mouth.

This is not to say that respect wasn't expected of our friends—of course it was—but it wasn't the bedrock of their childhoods the way it was ours. Sebastian broke this difference down for me: *Speaking to my mother in any kind of disrespectful tone was completely out the window. Cursing was completely out the window. It just didn't happen. I would realize the difference when I was over some of my friends' houses. The way they spoke to their parents was just nuts.*

All of us have experiences that underscore Sebastian's point, but of the ones I've heard, Will's is my favorite.

The episode took place in the den of his friend Zack's house. By his own admission, Will was a nerd then. Zack was too. They bonded over nerd stuff—Yu-Gi-Oh! cards and anime flicks, mostly. This particular Saturday afternoon, however, they paused their cross-cultural obsession to experiment with a more macho pursuit—billiards. Neither of them knew what they were doing, tying their fingers into generic gang signs on the table and sticking a cue through, scratching on the scant occasions they made contact at all. That's what Saturday afternoons were for, though, and the two laughed and joked as they plopped along.

Zack's younger brother heard the fun from above and, after a time, crept down to join them. He pestered the two friends in the way that little brothers do:

Hey, Zack, can I take a turn?
Come on guys, let me try!

Will empathized with the boy. Zack; less so. The two bickered, which elevated to an argument, and before long, a full-blown screaming match was in swing, with insults and dirty words whizzing 'round the room.

Mrs. Zack's Mom heard the commotion and came down next, but instead of entering the room, stopped at the foot of the stairs:

Zack, just be nice to Chris.

Zack kept his eyes locked on Chris:

Shut up, Mom.

Will flinched. His heart leapt. He held his breath and shut down motor function, *Cole, I was literally sitting there waiting for the frying pan to fly across the room.*

But instead, nothing happened. Mrs. Zack's Mom rolled her eyes, and the boys eventually quieted. Chris returned to his corner, and moments later, things settled to how they had been—two friends alternating errant pool shots.

Naturally, the armistice didn't last long. The gaiety below was too tempting for Chris to resist. The cycle began again. Prepubescent shrieking and name-calling, but this time nudges, and shoves, and fists as well. The two armed themselves with pool sticks—bob, weave, parry, strike, *crack*! Zack slammed the cue into Chris's spine causing the top half of the stick to splinter and ricochet away. Sniffling now, accompanied by sobbing, and shouting, and more name-calling. Then there was Mrs. Zack's Mom again with another round of soft pleas. Zack upped the ante:

Shut the fuck up, Mom.

Will still hadn't processed the first interaction. This one floored him: *At that point I'm sitting there like, "Whoa. This is insane. This shit is actually crazy." That same sequence of events with that same dialogue would not have been even remotely close to acceptable in my household.* The commotion did eventually quell for good, but Will was relieved when his mother finally showed up to retrieve him some time later. He high-fived Zack, thanked Mrs. Zack's Mom for having him, and scurried to the car, still hazy with confusion, not from the skirmish, but from its allowance.

I have stories nearly identical to Will's, as do most I know—times when we were present to one of our friends calling out four-letter words, or challenging authority in ways otherwise unimaginable. When asked how the parents of my token crew would've reacted to similar outbursts, responses varied from, *I would cease to exist,* to, *Ha! Boy I'd be kicked out that house before I squeezed the -itch syllable out my lips,* to, *My father would knock my head off.*

Maya's reaction to seeing a white friend act out was particularly poignant: *I was just completely and utterly shocked. Cole, if I had done that, you would have just never seen me again. I would have gotten the beatdown of the century and they would have just locked me in the basement after that. My parents just did not play that.*

Why did our parents uniformly enforce stricter constraints on us than our white counterparts? And why do I embrace those choices even more now, as I grow up and come to see the world with wiser eyes? Simply put, the stakes were and are higher for us.

This truth operated on two levels. The first was a risk of bodily harm that all Black parents, irrespective of environment, must be cognizant of. The rules that we kids interpreted as draconian were born of an anxiety, indeed an intractable fear, that our parents had of the unknown evils lurking in the crevices of a prejudiced world. That, for Black boys especially, carelessness needed to be corrected at home and at a young age. Should it be left unchecked, the physical cost in adulthood would prove a far higher price to pay.

Only with maturity did I come to recognize this anxiety for what it was. I look back today and see it scribbled across the rulebook Mama drafted for us, rules that seemed so arbitrary then. I remember buying my first flat-brimmed fitted cap in the eighth grade while mall-walking with a friend from grade school. The rappers I revered rocked them in the videos on *MTV Jams*, pulled low-to-the-brow with colorful du-rags spilling out the back. I wasn't allowed them, but I bought one anyway—an incredibly minuscule act of rebellion, in my view, that had an outsized impact on my level of cool. I successfully hid it in the back of my closet for weeks, stuffing it under my shirt when leaving the house only to don it once Ma had disappeared from sight. Eventually, she found it, of course—snatched it right off my head in front of company and whisked it away forever:

You're not walking out this house looking like a thug.

But Eric was allowed to keep his!

Well, I'm not Eric's Mom, am I?

Saggy pants and throwback jerseys faced the same rejection.

We didn't have a shoot-em-up video game, or so much as a water gun in the house, until I was well into my teenage years—Heaven forbid it inspire interest in, or be mistaken for, the real thing. I was in the tenth grade when Trayvon Martin was slain—a tragedy that threatened to uproot our home from its very foundations. His death ushered in a whole new wave of regulations. "The talk" played on repeat, tips on how best not to be converted to the past tense when interacting with figures of authority—legitimate or assumed. From then on, gatherings across town were met with extreme caution. Dark colors were discouraged. Hoodies were out entirely.

Mama warned me that the world would measure my manhood in inches rather than years; she measured my vulnerability in a commensurate fashion. She urged me not to rush to facial hair and other pubescent idols, for my claim on innocence had an early expiration date. I underwent a growth spurt in the eighth grade that pushed me past six feet and struck unmatched fear in her heart. Beginning in those months, every time I left our quiet neighborhood for some untamed territory, there was the same refrain:

Be careful, Cole.

Make good choices, Cole.

It only takes a second to cause a lifetime of trouble, Cole.

These were the slogans of anxiety—utterances of hope made in acknowledgment of her powerlessness to the persuasions of the wild. The threat of violence was real, and our parents did what they could to inculcate behaviors that would mitigate its reach. Such is the burden of Blackness—there is nothing particularly token about this experience—but its starkness was pronounced when placed next to the Erics of the world who were numb to the aroma of death on flat-brimmed caps.

But the high stakes of bad behavior operated on another level that was more particular to our environment. The fear of violence was ever-present, but it was tempered at times by the forgiving world we grew in. On days and nights when I remained in the microscopic bubble of affluence that was Chestnut Hill, Ma could heave a shallow sigh of relief that, if calamity was on the horizon, it *probably* wasn't arriving today. With that quiet consolation, she was free to turn her head to the more insidious actors attempting to influence my trajectory. Her myriad lectures on discipline and deference came from this place. For better or worse, I would always stand out among my peers. My mere presence would cause heads to turn. So, it was necessary to tread extra carefully while under the watchful eye of onlookers. Ma knew that insolence was a flaw that was interpreted entirely differently in Black men, and that the benefit of the doubt was a privilege I would have to fight for. She knew also that the time would come when the benefit of the doubt would be the difference between suspension and letting it slide, or acceptance and rejection. She refused to allow the one time I offended a middle-aged woman by calling her *Nina* to be the determining factor, no matter how unlikely the possibility was.

Will's example of hearing *Shut the fuck up* was, of course, extreme. Wildly extreme. But it exists on a wide spectrum of interactions that simply could not have occurred in my household, ranging from the seemingly mundane to the explicit and egregious. Maya labels this difference the *buddy-buddy* relationship she saw her white friends had with their parents. It was foreign to me too. The relationships with each of my parents have waxed and waned widely from nonexistent to symbiotic over the years, but even during pinnacles of connection, we have never been friends.

During my early childhood, Mama assumed the role of disciplinarian, which unfairly drove me closer to my father. I still remember evenings laying on his chest as a young boy, hearing the thump of his heart and yearning for the day that I'd have a strong chest to lay on with a strong heart to listen to, just like his. We had a bond of love and trust as deep as this earth had seen. Afternoons spent ascending his frame in a jumbled gaggle of contorted limbs before he could recover from work, only to fall to the floor once I'd summited. Sunday mornings, shaking sleep before the world to wrestle with mountain bikes through the park—McDonald's apple pies as a reward upon the completion of our voyage. We were close, but even then, I knew we weren't friends. He was father; I was son. Inherent in that relationship was a power gradient. I never confused our trust for parity.

When he left some years later, he took my deep adoration with him. Faith, Mama, and I were left to care for each other. I choke up when I think about how my mother handled those years. She navigated our ship through turbulent seas with unparalleled grace and stick-to-itiveness. His absence set off a cascade of transformation in our relationship. The disciplinarian-disciplined paradigm would no longer suffice; I was her oldest and she needed me. We grew together through those years, and with time I have evolved into a trusted advisor to my mother, a sounding board for her grand ideas, and even a confidant at times. We speak every day now, despite how life and opportunity have increased the distance between us. We are inseparable, but we aren't friends.

Neither of my parents desired to be my friend, a sentiment each expressed explicitly and often over the years. Consequences were swift and austere for children who forgot the dynamic at play. Respect was the foundation of our relationship, and even in youth I learned quickly not to trifle with that foundation.

Now, I don't want to give the false impression that my parents' approach kept me on the straight and narrow. I acquainted myself with mischief early, often, and just as much as, if not more than, any other child I knew: Black, white, blue, or purple. I flew too close to the sun, tumbled, then ascended again on a never-ending loop. But I was never disrespectful, that much they did accomplish.

The expectations they set made me bilingual from an early age. They taught me code-switching before I knew it had a name. The schoolyard, by day, had its own customs to impart, ones I naturally grew into. By night, my parents served as the backstop, counterbalancing those customs and *setting me straight*. They sent us off to the best education they could find, but when we returned, they worked to unravel those lessons they hadn't paid for. They retrained us for the world they knew awaited.

But their role was not only one of constraint; it was additive as well. Respect was the most fundamental element of their curriculum but was not the singular nor most important. They were constantly on the lookout for other realms where schooling would prove insufficient lessons for a Black kid growing up in America; seeking out ways to equip us fully for survival in this world.

I'm grateful for all of it. Even my old friends Leroy and Oscar.

———

In the fall of '05, NBA Commissioner David Stern announced a new dress code. The league would begin requiring players to dress in a suit and tie on their way to and from the arenas. Pundits dubbed it the *A. I. rule* after, who else but my hometown hero, Allen Iverson—the gold-chained, baggy-jeaned player thought to have inspired the policy. The move was hotly debated by sportscasters the world over, but as a third-grade soccer player, I couldn't have cared less. In fact, I hadn't even heard of the controversy the following day, bouncing about in the back row of the school bus, daydreaming while Philadelphia sports talk radio blared overhead. I drifted back to reality when their barking loudened. An authoritative voice leveled with me, *Let's be honest, they're really just trying to get these guys to dress white.*

These were the days before race pushed its way to the forefront, before I knew to notice that we lived in its shadow. I knew of it. I knew I was Black. I knew my classmates were white. I knew my parents were not my white friends' parents, for they often announced, *I'm not your white friends' parents!* But I didn't know it as I later would, as a personal, penetrating thing. Hearing the announcer's comment delivered with such authority, I knew that I agreed. I'd only seen few Blacks ever dressed in what Stern now required of his players, none outside our small circle of family and friends. The rest, those in the "out there," must have dressed like A. I.

My father arrived late that night and took time showering off the day's stresses. I listened for the drone of news anchors' voices to signal that he'd settled in, and when they did, I slinked into the bedroom and assumed my position next to him, overtop of the duvet. We began with small talk about the day and what I'd learned. The radio's pronouncement still ricocheting in my mind, I eventually mustered the courage to ask, *Dad, why do you dress white to work?*

My father jolted at the question. I rolled my gaze upward in time to separate the emotions as they crossed his face: bewilderment, anger, disappointment, determination. And perhaps, in the crow's feet corner, fear as well. There are precious few times in my life when I have seen my father at a loss for words. This was the first. To understand his reaction, you first have to have some understanding of him.

Payne Brown was Black on both sides. He grew up in a Fort Wayne that was just simmering from the height of the civil rights movement, riding the bus from his neighborhood to the white schools across town like all the other colored boys. His father, my Pop, traveled the country with the Equal Opportunity and Affirmative Action Office, while his mother, Helen Brown, simultaneously filled the roles of homemaker, barber, and community organizer. I never met Grandma Helen, but the lore of her time on Earth is well-told. She was a leader among our people in Fort Wayne, cutting hair for princes and paupers alike and maestro-ing city politics in her spare time. She served two terms as head of the local school board (a title she won over my father once, despite her refusing to campaign; voters just saw her name on the ballot and made the obvious choice). She was touched by cancer before we had the privilege of meeting—an event both of my parents regret as though they had a choice in the matter. When she fell, a natatorium was erected in her honor to commemorate a lifetime's worth of contributions to equality in education. Add to that stock a collection of character-defining run-ins with prejudice—my father was the director of public safety when crack hit, and he still regrets biting his tongue when his junior golf teammates dubbed his neighborhood Niggerville—and what you have is a Black identity that was fated to be fixed, firm, and well-fortified.

My question sent goose bumps to his Black flesh and dread to the marrow of his Black bones. With time, I came to appreciate the feeling of personal failure I must have thrust upon him—the realization that *his* son of all people assumed Black and professional to be mutually exclusive. His response came in a low, hushed tone with sober resolve,

Son, this is exactly the type of shit I can't have you buying into. You need to be free.

I stammered an *okay* without any understanding of my offense. Then, I slipped out of the room when he began to nod away.

I'd all but forgotten the exchange by the time the garage's rustlings announced he'd returned home again the following day. Before I could leap from my room to greet him, I heard the clink of the backdoor latch and his heavy footsteps pummeling the front stairs. Soon, he was in my entryway—furrowed brow and a weighty plastic bag sagging by his side. He entered, strode to the foot of my bed, and turned the bag upside down, unleashing a flood of a dozen or more books that tumbled down with a thud and a bounce.

These are your people. You are going to read all of these. Each time you finish one, I want you to write a report in this. . . .

He handed me a black leather journal with gold-rimmed pages. He paused for a moment, but his expectant glare awaited affirmation, not negotiation. I nodded my head, then he turned and left the room as briskly as he'd entered.

I gawked at the mound before me. Stacked on end, these books measured taller than I did—a gajillion pages each, at least. What did he mean, *all of them*?? I envisioned myself withering away a century later, shakily turning the final pages of book #1. Minutes of stalling and ogling passed, then I sifted through the covers. One had the image of a smiling, light-skinned, Black man in thick, horn-rimmed glasses on its cover with *Thurgood*

Marshall emblazoned in bold letters across the front. Another, the thickest of the lot, had the title *The Autobiography of Malcolm X* printed above a cartoonish sketch of a grave man. Quickly, I scanned the others: *Narrative of the Life of Frederick Douglass; The Collected Poems of Langston Hughes; I Know Why the Caged Bird Sings; The Souls of Black Folk.* There were names that rung a familiar bell, and others I had to work my mouth around to get right. I settled on a book called *Black Boy*, an utterly random selection, and so embarked on an exploration into my people.

Months of frustration followed. I was a reader, but a lover of fantasy and adventure. My people had doldrums and sluggishness to share. I wasted more than one potential bike-riding, tree-climbing afternoon on book reports. Still, I worked my way through. I can't say I finished the whole stack that crashed onto the comforter that evening, but I made a good dent. By fourth grade, I'd read the autobiographies of Malcolm X and Frederick Douglass, as well as a biography of Justice Marshall, Richard Wright's seminal work, and nearly half the canon of Langston Hughes.

Dad constructed his curriculum in response to a question only the parents of tokens needed consider. For all the benefits their hard work had provided, of which there were many, a quintessential part of our identity was missing. From where would we learn about Blackness? Certainly not from our formal education, which tiptoed around our history eleven months of the year, slowing only briefly to play Dr. King's greatest hits during February's twenty-eight short days. Certainly not from the young children we'd mature alongside, for whom we would be the sole exposure to the melanin pigment and for whom MTV would be the primary provider of its connotation. Even our Black classmates could not be counted upon, for it would be years before they were drawn into our fold in critical mass, long after they'd already grown warmly into their own Blackness. If not them, then who?

Our parents needed to shoulder that burden.

Enlightened minds could disagree over how to confront the responsibility, but to avoid it altogether would be a tragic dereliction. Bas came to know Blackness on Saturday mornings during basketball clinics at his local Baptist church, even though he preferred to draw. His mom half-jokingly told him he'd have to *give up his Black card* if he stayed home, underscoring the importance of *learning how to interact with brothas.* Ma dragged Faith to Jack and Jill outings on Sundays for her encounter with Blackness, though death seemed to her a better alternative.

For us all, the lessons meant playdates with kids whom we had little in common with, other than that we were the only brown faces sharing our lower-school homerooms. We all had stories of those forced relationships with the children of our parents' friends—kids who we couldn't stand to be around but who, we were continually reassured, would prove a treasured relationship later on in life.

Then, of course, there was my personal version of the encounter—reading the works of my predecessors. The texts did not have the effect my father hoped they would, at least not initially. The nuances of the literature that made it worth reading soared far above my head. The few concepts I did understand, I stored and filed away as ancient history. It would be years before I could look out to the world and recognize those abstract themes, made tangible.

A few of the details stick with me today. I recall Bigger Thomas thrashing poor Bessie off into eternity. I recall Earl Little, Malcolm's father, falling victim to the white mob. When young, it was the graphic violence that struck me, not the truth beyond it. What I did gain was a peek into a whole literary tradition that would've otherwise remained obscured from view. Black leaders were seldom discussed in my all-white classrooms, if ever. The pages of those books carried the Black experience, curated by men and women with the most intimate of relationships with it. Their works were time capsules, preserving the aspirations and frustrations of generations. The reading assignments sowed the seeds of skepticism that I would need to survive in this world of promise, though I would not realize it until many years later.

Today, years from fatherhood, the long limbs of anxiety stretch out to me, faintly brushing my bristles. I know both of my parents must have felt its strangulating clutch when some MD excitedly proclaimed, *it's a boy!* Alongside the joyful bubbliness, there must have been a tremendous weight—the responsibility of raising a Black man to confront the injustice of a white world; disillusioning a Black boy to the myth of equality, without robbing him of his childhood innocence; passing along wisdom but not baggage. My father did what he could, and when he fell at a loss for words, he invoked the musings of our forebears.

When the awkward struggles of middle school came, and all became aware of race at once, I suddenly felt very Black sitting in those classrooms. I tumbled and flailed and nearly met my end. But the lifeline I grabbed onto, the one that dragged me from the swirling cyclone, was authored by mystics who'd plumbed deeper depths than I'd ever come to know. They told of how black Blackness could get and how bright as well. They insisted upon my worth, and their generations became the pedestal I learned to balance upon.

*Confusion is a luxury which only the very, very young can possibly
afford and you are not that young anymore.*

—James Baldwin

To a Friend I Almost, Kind Of, Once Had

Dear Kamryn,

I owe you an apology. I didn't do right by you all those years ago when we were in middle school, before you transferred away, and I did too. We haven't spoken in the years since; in fact, I would be unsurprised to learn that you have forgotten me entirely. But I haven't forgotten you. Though I can only imagine you as you were then—small frame, dark skin, short hair you tied back or wove braids upon. Back then, you were bubbly—your whole body shivered when you giggled. Somehow, I still know that even though I barely knew you. These days, I reflect on our brief encounters (few in number) and nonencounters (many more) and can't help but feel a pang of guilt. It comes with the knowledge that you deserved better.

I can't remember where we met but I know where we didn't meet. We didn't meet at ballroom dancing class in the third grade, which is where I first met your future classmates, a number of whom you would be similarly forgiven for having forgotten by now. You weren't there, and while I've never asked, I imagine that is in part because you weren't a member of the Philadelphia Cricket Club. I know this because my family would soon join the Philadelphia Cricket Club and I'd spend countless afternoons sipping drinks named after dead white people by the pool at the Philadelphia Cricket Club and if there was a Black girl of my age (of any age) that was a member of the Philadelphia Cricket Club, I'd know. I imagine also that you didn't attend because it was a totally unneeded extravagance with slim hope of any return on investment.[12] I was there, however. So were a whole gaggle of soon-to-be pot smokers and suspensioneers— my friends. So, too, was the Lilly Pulitzer–clad clan that would claim you as their BFFL. We strolled over in posses from our separate campuses after school, boys-with-boys and girls-with-girls, got suited and booted, and received instruction on an off-beat foxtrot—*one, two, th-th-three, f-four.* But as I'm sure you well know, or once knew, none of the children went to dance class to dance. We went to integrate.

The Springside School for Girls was a dozen steps from ours, fixed in the land of the unknown. We boys had heard of the beings that dwelled there—like us, but not. Like our mothers and sisters, but very not. You trotted along a pattered path in that

---

12   It was also, admittedly, some excessively white, white-people shit.

floating enigma. It was the same path that my sister traveled along a few years behind you. Parallel to the path that I was on at the time, until the two of them converged, and then we both hopped off. It was a path reserved for the representative peoples. James Choy was on it next to me. For you and him and Faith and I weren't one-of; in the circles we ran in, we were the only. During the "pre-race era," when kids were kids were kids, to the extent that such an era ever existed at all, we were the Black sheep in the play pen (James was a half-Asian sheep). That is until the outer edges of those circles began to blur, and bend, and rupture, and middle school arrived.

Kids weren't kids anymore in middle school. Kids were assets and liabilities. There was cellular division and reorganization, and casualties were created in the mitosis. You and I survived though, even if just barely, and our same-sex groups began to drift in each other's direction, slowly at first, then rushing like time was short. We gathered at mutually agreed upon times and locations; the fortunate few among us with Facebooks and cell phones were anointed organizers.

Are the girls going to Friday night skate?

Will the boys be at the dance?

Always a single, gendered unit and always pre-established—contact was too crucial to be left to chance. Once together, we transgressed just outside of parental sightlines. First hand-holds and first kisses. First boners and first-of-many embarrassments. First relationships with week-long sunsets. It was innocent, of course, but it all rung hot like sinful taboo. Before long, people were pairing off like Noah's zoo. Like a draft board. Like with like.

I don't know that we'd met, but it was around this time that I became aware of you. Your name was popping up everywhere suddenly. We were pawns in the same plot. Plans were drawn, and communiqués were back-channeled through third parties:

Do you think Kam likes Cole? Amber told Brittany that she heard from Alexa that she like-likes him.

What does Cole think of Kam? Lauren said he's in loooooooove.

Your friends were Cupid's emissaries, approaching me with their palms open skyward.

Who am I gonna tell?

What a stupid question.

Their awkward schemes are still fresh to me. Do you remember spending one Friday as guests at Pub Night—family night for that country club in the nearby 'burbs, when all the kids slipped away to practice flirtation on the golf course? The whispers bubbled immediately, and the matchmaking followed shortly thereafter. Suggestive glares and concocted queues.

Do you remember the group running from us, shutting the nighttime and forest behind them? We were left in a gentle spotlight to fidget and breathe. I don't know what sort of romance novel drama was expected of that moment "alone," but I'm sure we disappointed them, the investors in our romance.

You weren't interested in me. Nothing personal. I think you *liked* me, but Alexa miscalculated when she added the second *like*. I seem to remember you having your eyes on the Bieber haircut to my right, who, in turn, had his eyes on the Barbie doll to your left. I wasn't interested either—dumb Lauren. My eyes were all over the damn place but narrowing their focus on Willow, another member of your crew. To us both, the pairing felt forced. We didn't even know each other! We'd hardly spoken. No matter. No one was about to let the facts get in the way of a union so . . . logical.

On weekdays, back in testosterone territory, the boys were as nagging as anything I can imagine the girls were.

Dude, you're totally into it, bro (hah). Stop being a pussy and just go for it already (hahahaha).

It was all a big joke punctuated with knowing nods and shoulder punches. I was the ass of it. I couldn't have that, could I? I had a rep to protect. I had a rep to erect. So, I did what came most naturally; I met their claims with defiance. I strung together too many *ewwww*'s and *never-would-I-ever*'s to count. I regret that now. It was a defense mechanism. But I was too young, too immature, to see the game we were playing.

The first inkling of understanding came some months later, when I was crushing hard on an older girl—a big, bad high schooler who was big sister to one of my classmates. She was stunning, with a combination of features that seemed to be plucked at random out of a genetic hat: fair-skinned, freckle-faced, gap-toothed, curly-haired. But she pulled it all off in a way that was both perfect and inescapably Black. Mine was the kind of fleeting infatuation that all young boys have for their friends' older siblings. The kind that strikes as a flutter of blows, over-and-over-and-over again, adding up to an era of general, unrequited lustfulness, but otherwise lost to time.

I was on Instant Messenger one night (remember Instant Messenger?) gloating about this new crush of mine as if I had something to gloat about—as if she was proof of my unimpeachable taste, as if my taste was *responsible* for her perfection—to one of your classmates whom I considered a friend—a white girl whose friendship dissipated not long after you left. I was slipping into monologue when she cut me short:

You can't be talking about her. She's gross.

I chuckled. I must not have heard her correctly.

No seriously, Cole. What the hell are you talking about? She's disgusting!

It is a strange experience hearing an otherwise sane person—someone whose judgement you know firsthand to be sound—say something so totally and completely not sane. All sorts of thoughts jumble together and assert themselves:

She'swrong.Isshewrong?AmIwrong?There'samiscommunication. This idiot.AmIwrong?Nosheis.Right?

I closed the laptop shortly thereafter and strode to my parents' room, where the TV watched my father, half asleep. I poked him awake and fell into exasperated verbal vomit.

I don't get it. I just don't get it, Dad. I'll show you her. Look at her, Dad! She's pretty! Really, really pretty! I think she's sooo pretty. Please look. I guess it's okay to think she's not beautiful. But gross? How could she say that? What is she thinking? I just don't get it.

It wasn't the fundamental inaccuracy, it was the terminology:

gross, disgusting, words reserved for spoiled artichokes and dark alcoves of the Internet, that shook me. The seed was planted. These scales were imbalanced.

It took Faith aging for me to understand the extent of that imbalance (as fully as I'm capable anyway). I'm not proud of that fact. I remember when it was Faith's turn to go to Pub Nights and flirt with flirtation. I remember also the years that soon followed. I watched her friends grow into themselves. Less stringy now. More sparkle and gleam. Faith grew too, but differently. She curled in places they were board-straight and rounded at their angles. She blossomed, accentuating a light, a warmth, that she'd always had. It intensified with age, pulling people into her orbit. But would she see it? Would she recognize her light, its luster and allure?

I knew how hard it would be for her, 'cause I'd seen it before. I remembered those white boys who told me they *just aren't into Black chicks*—the same white boys who Black and white chicks alike straightened up for when they crossed the hallways. I remembered my Lax Bro buddy, pre–Black Table, who described my interest in our kind, your kind, as an odd fetish. I remembered how I, your male counterpart, fed on their opinions, and perpetuated a broken narrative that regarded you as lesser. I remembered also the sorry souls I had known who stumbled through the pubescent years drunk on anguish, crushed by fruitless crushes.

Then I remembered you.

I had a front row seat when you went through it. I went

through it with you. I watched them devalue (undervalue) your beauty. Label you undesirable and treat it as a forgone conclusion, indeed as a generally accepted premise. As Common Wisdom. Scientific, even. You weren't the only one. They did it to many over the years. But you were the first.

I don't have the slightest idea how you processed the whispers—how/if/when you managed to eke out an appreciation of your worth. It's hard out here for a Black girl. Harder still for a Black girl in a white world. I know I don't have to tell you that, Kam. I certainly had a hard enough time as a Black boy. I too know how unworthiness feels. I'm sorry I didn't step in to remind you of your glory.

I expect that you're on to wondrous things now. Teenage gossip cuts shallow, biting wounds. Most recover. My sister is doing well today. So is the sister of my then-classmate. They both found a place of their own in that chaos; found principles and boundaries and a plot in this universe to stake out and claim. It makes them special, not unique. They give me confidence that you're excelling, by your own standards if not theirs. I hope you're told you matter by those who matter to you. If not, my line's always open.

With Gratitude,
Cole

THE GREAT ONES

FAMILY AND *LA FAMILIA* made me, but Francis Ford Coppola had his say. My father seeded a love for the man's cinematic triumphs when I was still much too young to watch along. He established a Thanksgiving tradition in our household early on. Once we'd glutted our guts, we waddled off to the living room. There, we watched *The Godfather Part I*, and if we could stave off the drowsiness, *Part II* as well. Dad crashed before Michael's ascension. My eyes stretched wide for the end credits. With time, my obsession blossomed to include the whole mob genre, the classics most of all. It has fed me a well of otherwise useless knowledge. It is possible that a scenario exists for which a *Godfather* quote is not appropriate, but I have yet to come across one.[13]

---

13   I can't shake the feeling that those films romanticized Italians for the same depraved behavior that begets my peoples' demonization. Serious flaw, no doubt. But that notwithstanding, I am a mafioso Stan.

Despite their obvious shortcomings (sociopathy for one, and vehement, seemingly bottomless racism for another) those silver screen gangsters displayed a vision of manhood that I valued.[14] I saw my father in them and vice versa—the heavy seriousness they lugged, their quiet confidence, their unrelenting cool in the face of torment: *never tell anyone outside the family what you're thinking.* They were calculated to the point of clairvoyance. The most fearsome of those antiheroes had hardened themselves against all weakness and illogic. They were rocks parting rushing rapids.

Behind *The Godfather*, which is objectively the greatest film ever created, my favorite of the genre is the tragically underappreciated *A Bronx Tale*—a "coming of age story" in the truest and least cliché possible sense of the phrase. The movie follows Calogero—C, as he comes to be known—a Bronx-born baby boomer torn between his union-made father and Sonny, the mobster next door. The movie is thick with that lovely mafia-brand morality and 1960s Americana—barbershop doo-wop, stickball, Mickey Mantle-this-and-that, and a bright red Cadillac DeVille for the Maraschino cherry. *A Bronx Tale* stands apart from the mob-movie pack. It scarcely concerns itself with the schemes of scoundrels. Instead, it's all C, and his evolution in a world that crime built.

In his teenage years, C finds himself hopelessly in like with Jane Williams—a classmate of his at the local high school. It is just as tongue-twisting and gut-pummeling as first crushes are

---

14   Should I ever find myself running for president or under indictment, I will assuredly disavow this last sentence.

supposed to be—C turns all starry eyes and butterflies. He's unsure what to do. He brings his dilemma to Sonny, who coats kernels of wisdom in elaborate wrappings of street vernacular and mid-century sensibilities as only a Hollywood mob boss can:

You gotta do what your heart tells you to do. Let me tell you somethin' right now. You're only allowed three great women in your lifetime. They come along like the great fighters, every ten years. Rocky Marciano. Sugar Ray Robinson. Joe Louis. Sometimes you get 'em all at once. Me? I had my three when I was sixteen. That happens. What are you gonna do? That's the way it goes, you know? Tell you right now. See this girl? Maybe this girl, she put wind in your sails. Maybe she's your first Great One. . . .

C nods along, wide-eyed at the wisdom he's found. He treats Sonny's advice as gospel. How could he not? *This could be one of the Great Ones.* All told, the guidance proves useful. We never discover what the future holds for the two, but their final moments hint at happiness.

But does their happyish ending confirm Sonny's hypothesis? Are we meant to conclude that he was right? I certainly hope not.

You're only allowed three great women in your lifetime.

Please God, let Sonny be wrong.

———

The first Great appeared in the third grade. Ballroom dancing class. Golden hair and waxen skin. Pink blushed cheeks to match her rose-hued lips. Her name was Willow Carter.

Willow was churlish in childhood; she stepped on her

partners' toes without remorse. In the locker room, barely out of earshot, we boys teased her endlessly for it, invented puns for her wintry heart. We'd all been raised as princes of our respective castles and couldn't resist fascination with the first to treat us as anything less than. I couldn't have known it then, of course, but some years later, she'd be the one to check off my landmark firsts—first crush, first date, first to spur me to thinking I knew something of the shape of love. The nearly five-year saga we embarked on consumed my little heart whole.

We forged a relationship early in middle school, when all first learned of the other sex. When our crews came together, we found our reasons to sit separate and near. By eighth grade, we called each other *best friend,* yet quietly held hopes of morphing to more. With the start of ninth grade, *more* had become inevitable.

Christmas spirit was waning, and Valentine's Day was just poking into view when I asked her to be my girlfriend. Her birthday fell during that comforting sliver of the year, so after thorough consultation with Mama and Faith—the brain trust—I purchased a small, silver necklace with a curlicue "w" pendant to mark the completion of her fifteenth year and the beginning of our first.

The day before I was to ask her, I sat in the car with my father, traversing Chestnut Hill. It'd only been months since he moved out, but already our interactions had dumbed—*How's high school? How are your teachers? What are your friends up to?* blahblahblah. I'd kept the necklace on my person since buying it. It seared a curlicue brand into my thigh. He didn't ask, but I couldn't resist:

I think I'm going to ask Willow to be my girlfriend tomorrow.

Who?

Willow, Dad. You've met before.

The white girl?

Yes . . . the white girl.

The one I met at . . . ?

Yeah, that one.

You sure?

I was, but his was not a question of resolve. What he really meant, the real question behind *You sure?*, I hadn't heard before. By the time Willow and I were through, I'd be greeting it as an old friend:

Ain't there any Black girls you can date instead?

Dad's reaction was not Sonny's, though Willow was my Jane. For Jane Williams, the apple of C's proverbial eye, was Black. Beautifully so. With flawless supple skin and tightly laid baby hairs. Jane sauntered with a calm confidence that was light-years beyond anything her peacocking complements could muster, and when she side-eyed C from the back of the bus in an early scene, my own heart hiccupped. The poor boy didn't stand a chance.

But C was Italian, surrounded by Italians, and living in the sixties. His 'hood anointed Blacks with epithets and sent them on their way. For anyone else in his crew, race would've trivialized all Jane's many perfections. But not C. Jane stirred his desires despite the prejudice he'd known. He sought Sonny's guidance while at a loss for next steps—to advance or retreat? And how would he face his friends with a *colored broad* on his arm? Sonny was characteristically blunt:

Fuck them. Half of them are gonna end up dead or in jail. Nobody cares. Only thing that matters is what's good for you and how you feel about each other. . . . You gotta do what your heart tells you to do.

Sonny responded with understanding, nobility even, and despite his obvious failings, appeared to have his feet firmly planted on the side of right. The moment was warm and fuzzy and fictitious. The writers' room wrapped Sonny's fictional frame in contrived complexity. You mean to tell me that an Italian American mobster living in the 1960s Bronx would push his pseudo-son toward the warmth of a Black embrace? Give me a break.

Fortunately, C's real father, Lorenzo, swooped in to rescue us from comforting mismemory. With Lorenzo, C masked his inquiry in anticipation of the inevitable:

I need your opinion. You know Joey Osso from down the block?

Yeah.

He asked me what I thought about him going out with a colored girl. What do you think about that?

Joey can't find any white girls?

Ah, now that's more like it. There's the down-home, apple-pie-prejudice I'm owed. Simple and to the point. The moment deserved Lorenzo's response, if for no other reason than because it was honest. In the lives of the tokens I know, our Lorenzos outnumbered the Sonnys by a long shot.

Jackson Patterson is a blueprint of token design. We've known each other for years and I have only ever seen him in a pair of Sperry Top-Siders, khaki shorts, and an incredibly ill-fitting, pastel polo shirt. Son of a banker and an insurance entrepreneur, Jackson attended the Peddie School, an elite Northeastern boarding school, for his high school years. He went on to play D1 lacrosse at Colgate, spending three years on its roster before becoming the team's first ever Black captain. Jackson makes his presence known; he's loud and boisterous. Ask anyone from a certain set of schools in the Northeast corridor if they know him and they'll respond with puzzlement. Add that he's *the Black lacrosse player at Colgate* and, invariably, *Oooohhhh I know Jackson!* becomes the answer. Aside from his more stereotypically WASPy biographical details, Jackson is also one of the most woke and clear-headed individuals I've ever had the pleasure of knowing.

Jackson's alma mater is a small liberal arts school positioned smack in the center of New York State, deep in the heart of Whiteville (Great Migrationers hung a U-turn well before making it to this particularly frigid region of our country). It's not difficult to imagine Jackson spending days, weeks even, bouncing between small class sizes and lacrosse practice, interacting almost, if not totally, exclusively with white people. He was a Black student playing a white sport at a white school in a white part of the country—tokenism in its most extreme iteration.

Sophomore year surfaced a young woman from that porcelain pond who shook Jackson to attention. Their paths crossed briefly that spring at a neighborhood bar. When he stepped to speak to her, *you're really smart*, was all he could muster before disappearing to the din. They shared a kiss in a frat house some weeks after that too, but as his first year of college wound down, Jackson couldn't honestly count the girl as much more than an acquaintance.

In time, he would learn that she was Annabelle from St. Louis, the soon-to-be president of Kappa Kappa Gamma with eyes on a career in law. His second fall semester was colored by their magnetism and punctuated by another kiss at the lacrosse formal—they went arm-in-arm as dates. As Christmas break rolled in, Annabelle had a confession to make:

I want you to be my boyfriend.

Jackson felt the timing was odd. In a matter of hours, she'd be flying to the Midwest and he'd be returning to New Jersey. Was a month apart really the way to start their relationship?

Can we talk about this after break?

Okay, I'm just scared you're going to come back, start your lacrosse season, and you're not really gonna want to . . . you'll get busy and this is just gonna die.

We like each other, so it'll work itself out. We'll figure it out.

They retreated to their respective residences then returned in January to the same heap of uncertainty they'd discarded in December. He caught a glimpse of Annabelle in a bar during their first week back. A younger teammate had her cornered, trying and failing to conjure seduction with clumsy gestures and boozy breath. Jackson made his way over:

Hey man, I see you met my girlfriend.

Your what? Annabelle blurted out.

All he could do was smile in return. She smiled too, then nuzzled a bit closer. His teammate faded away and it was just the two of them left, which is how it would be for the next three years.

With spring came the beginning of lacrosse season, which meant family visits and a chance for Annabelle to meet the parents. Jackson had told them he was seeing a girl. He'd mentioned she was white. But that was it. The formal introduction finally came after the Lehigh game. Annabelle sat in the stands, only a few feet away from the Patterson parents, but waited for her beau to make the introduction.

Mom, Dad, meet Annabelle. Annabelle, this is my mom and dad.

Nice to meet you.

Nice to meet you.

Nice to meet you.

Nice to meet you.

They chatted for a moment before parting ways. As Annabelle floated off, Jackson remembers his mother's curt, stiff *hmm.* That's all she had to say. *Hmm.* He thought to himself, *What the hell does hmm mean?* But he decided against responding. He let it go.

When he returned home that summer, little things continued to bother him. A cousin's name once came up in conversation and his mom interjected:

Oh, you know he dates that white girl, right?

Once, Annabelle was the topic and Mrs. Patterson chimed in: *Yeah, yeah Jackson, she's cute.*

Factual, but not flattering.

She knew he dated a white girl. He knew she knew he dated a white girl. He thought to himself, *If you love me, Mom, and you know I'm happy and clearly in love with this girl, then why would you say all these things that were anti our relationship?*

His mother's reactions may seem minor, but consider the leap of faith required to introduce the heretofore most important woman in his life to her newest challenger for the belt. Particularly as men—Black men—rarely do we place ourselves in so emotionally vulnerable a position. It would be hard to overstate the importance of a mother's approval on that matter. *Hmm* was all Jackson needed to know he hadn't earned his.

His predicament rang a familiar tone. I knew that feeling by then. *Cute* was Mrs. Patterson's euphemism of choice. *You sure?* was my father's. It all meant the same thing—*Ain't there any Black girls you can date instead?* Neither ever suggested an outright ban on white partners, but the subtle aspersions cut deep—deep enough to make one reconsider his course.

Jackson tired of being on the defensive. He felt that judgement swirled around him at home and couldn't find much reprieve out in the world either. He remembered boarding a New York subway with Annabelle. She laid her hand on his thigh as they rode, patting the intimate real estate between warm and erotic. Across from them sat a woman whose expression read disgust. Her eyes met Jackson's for a fleeting moment of disdain, before she snorted and peered back at her phone. *Annabelle didn't notice it—why would she?—but it really, really bothered me.*

Even close friends, fellow tokens at that, shared their disapproval. Messages came to his phone regularly: a Facebook snapshot coupled with *Why is she calling you honey?* or an Instagram DM that read, *Does she have to flaunt her whiteness?*

Peer pressure; that too was familiar to me. My position at the Black Table had been cemented by the time Willow and I were off and running, but let relationships come up and the Great Debaters had a trump card I couldn't match:

Oh, shut up nigga, you know you only like white bitches.

Not factual. Cut to the bone.

Jackson's frustration crested in short order. One year into his relationship with Annabelle, Jackson found himself in love. Deeply in love. This-might-be-the-last-girl-ever in love. But the *hmms* kept coming. Finally, he spoke up:

Mom, it just hurts when you make backhanded remarks about people in interracial relationships, knowing full well that I'm in love with a white girl. I don't understand why you can't just support that when clearly, I'm happy.

As Jackson spoke, tears pooled in the corners of his eyes until their weight was too heavy to dam. Then Mrs. Patterson cried too:

I never wanted you to feel that way. I wasn't doing it on purpose, but you have to understand that, for me, it hurts me to see you with her.

How could that hurt you?

Son, you got all this love from a Black woman, so for you to go out and find love from a woman who doesn't look like me. . . . It's like a stab to my heart.

Mom, I really wish you didn't look at it that way because the two of you are more alike than even a lot of the Black women I know. If you actually get to know her, you'll see that you're more similar than you understand.

Mrs. Patterson apologized to her son and promised she'd try. And try she did. She spent time with Annabelle and, in the short term at least, Jackson was right. The two of them hit it off. They bridged the obvious differences and reached the more significant similarities beyond. Jackson's relationship with Annabelle continued to blossom as well. For a time, it looked as though his last-girl-ever visions might come to pass.

A harbinger of their demise waved its hand the summer after Jackson's junior year. He, like so many of his classmates, migrated to New York City to toil at the lowest rung of the banking ladder. Until then, he'd spent a lifetime between prep schools and PWIs, frat parties, and dive bars. But New York was something else. New York was new, hot, alive. New York was freedom-laden concrete and steel. New York had Black people everywhere. Saturdays were La Marina up in Harlem. Sundays were Everyday People down in Brooklyn. Jackson found brothers on that dance floor when the DJ played "Swag Surf." And the women. The Women. Every size, shape, and shade you could imagine were out there strutting their stuff or repping their colors. Septum piercings and combat boots linked up with perms and sundresses to vibrate to Afrobeats. Let Juvenile's "Back That Ass Up" come on in the party and even the most faithful man was tempted.

He sensed something out there that he was missing. Something that Annabelle couldn't provide. Something that he needed. A creeping feeling gnawed at him. They tottered along together for months, but the shadow of doubt clung to his heels. He surrendered. Soon after graduation, they split.

New York presented Jackson a brief glimpse into the world of Black love. It exposed something unique and irresistible. It left him spellbound. He saw women whose very being had been forged by melanin in ways that his own had been—ways that his mother had an appreciation of long before he did. Jackson left New York that summer with an inching suspicion that a Black woman could understand and nourish him in ways that nobody else, not even Annabelle, would be capable of.

And you know what? He was right. There is something uniquely profound about Black women. My existence is evidence of the nearly divine capabilities of at least three of them—Faith, Mama, and Grandma Marta. And I would be remiss not to add to that list the many aunties and teachers and Ms. So-and-sos who had a hand in molding me. I have borne witness to their power and grace firsthand, the full extent of which defies description and demands wonder. Only a special kind of fool could look upon that strength and not long to see it replicated in an equal.

Years on from those final moments he and Annabelle shared, Jackson is today happy. He moved to New York for his first post-grad gig and floated further away into the dating pool. He frequented dinners and drinks and comedy shows and walks in the park with girls whose social circles intersected his own. They were recent graduates from great schools who were out there in the big city trying to figure things out like he was. They were Black like he was.

Soon, he collided with someone special. He witnessed the fruits of his mother's wisdom come to bear. Her name is Sydney. He found himself a Great One and knew enough not to let her go. His mother is ecstatic, and he appears to have taken her words to heart—always a good move.

It took few months for their attraction to bloom beyond petty puppy love. He and Sydney relate on the matters that matter to them both in the here and now. They're side by side traversing this unchartered, adult world. He needn't translate when speaking of struggles with familial or corporate life. She sees it and lives it herself. They love unfiltered, calling out *nigga!* in times of ecstasy and strife—a seemingly trivial, yet novel, emblem of freedom that he's grown to embrace.

He met her parents for the first time and fell nerve-racked in ways altogether different than his reaction to Annabelle's. He carried the same pit of insecurity with him, one that stuttered his diction and perspired his palms in the same way, but it bubbled up from a different wellspring. This nervousness was plucked from an eighties teen movie. It wrapped him in his role as *new boyfriend*, not in his identity as *Black man*. It was a temporary thing, easily massaged away, not rooted in the weight of uncertainty he'd lugged for a lifetime. They laughed over Chris Rock jokes and in fifty minutes he'd fallen into their fold. Even more so than affection, he felt alleviation.

Jackson treasures the time he shared with Annabelle. But he feels also that the man he is today and the man he will be going forward, could only ever be with a Black woman, for there are parts of him that only a Black woman could possibly understand.

Life unveiled to him a doctrine on Black love that his mother likely arrived at decades earlier. Hearing him today, the wisdom he shares is so very familiar—an iteration of a conversation I have had on occasions too numerous to number. With adults, often: parents, aunties, and so on. At times, with peers like Jackson as well. They mush together in my mind, dialogues that so often take the same form. That is, except for one: an exchange with a young woman who pushed me to the edges of my soundest reasoning and then beyond.

I met her on a Chicago rooftop in the year following my graduation from Georgetown. We gritted our teeth through the still frigid air, insisting, beyond all evidence to the contrary, that surely May marked rooftop season. I was there to connect with Nikki, an old friend from college, and the coworker she'd brought along, a woman whose name I don't now recall, which is strange, given the striking impression she instilled. We were the same age, but she was more buttoned-up than I, more restrained, not speaking as freely as she seemed capable. That would, however, soon change.

They told me about office life, and I lamented Chicago

winters. We caught up the way one-time friends do. Then, seeking a dismissal of pleasantries, the conversation turned to dating lives.

What's your type, Cole?

Short answer: *I have no idea.* The few I'd grown close to had
sparse discernable similarities. Intelligent, kind, open-minded:
broad-reaching specifications that limit my pool to most good,
interesting people. Race was not listed.

So you date white girls?

Short answer: *I have*—bait I bit. Nikki laughed, *you sure you
want to do this, Cole?* She knew both her friend and I well; she
sensed the quarrel as it brewed. But there ain't no stopping a
train that's left the station. I wouldn't backtrack. We tumbled
into a conversation I knew well. She opened with a familiar suite
of charges. My responses were well-rehearsed. We went back-
and-forth, blow-for-blow. A half hour in, neither of us showing
signs of fatigue, she approached from an unexpected angle:

*We have such deep love for you, for all of you, for all of our men.
We are on the front lines when the world comes down on y'all, fighting,
shedding tears, risking our lives, all for y'all, even when you don't do
the same for us. We march and protest when police kill y'all. Nobody
says a word when we fall. Yet, still we love. So, it hurts, Cole. It hurts
when, after all that, you won't support us the way we support you—
won't love us the way we love you.*

What could I say?

I couldn't tell her she was wrong. I knew the same examples
she did—celebrities who'd settled white and Benedict Arnold

Blacks who spoke ill of our sisters. I knew the statistics, that we Black men were twice as likely to find marriage outside our race. Even more so for those with college degrees. She must've known I knew. My expression would've told her even if my words didn't. The woman who looked back at me wasn't emotional; she was fed up. And it showed.

I stammered and paused. I scrambled to beat back her charges. But as I grasped for knowledge to call upon, all that emerged was my own life, and the many ways it could've fixed insecurity within me.

I remembered Savannah Sincova, Sav, one of my closest friends during my Penn Charter days. Sav was from a working class, take-no-shit part of Philly that was emblematic of, and responsible for, the stereotype. She had the drawl to prove it— our oceans were made of *wooder* and the second-person plural pronoun was *yous*, as in: *Yous tailgating the Eagles game today?* for which there was only ever one answer. We suffered the same after-school SAT-prep class side by side and it drew us close to one another.

I remembered how Sav, often with the same breath, shared her affection for me and her disinterest in Black men. That she could never see herself settling with one. She'd look past my brown nose and into my brown eyes to say it. She did so without shame, which could've served as a small conciliatory acknowledgment of her backwardness. She did so without pride, which could've confirmed her malice. She reported it factually. Uncontroversially. And often accompanied the observation with a slight shudder that read, *heebie-jeebies*, as if relegating an entire race of people to the realm of the unworthy was a personality quirk as endearing as all others.

Many of the white kids I knew were on the spectrum that Sav anchored. In the course of picking partners, they cordoned us Black kids off as other. They fetishized, or objectified, or kept at arms distance and held their noses like *pee-yew*. I knew the seed of bias, conscious or otherwise, that rejection could sow. The interactions I shared with them lent credence to Nikki's friend, and Jackson's mom, and that subway rider seated opposite the happy couple.

I saw the truth in Nikki's friend's point of view, but then I remembered Willow and had to all at once reject the choice as it was framed. As binary. As zero-sum. As a choice at all. I remembered those first exchanges, drifting from pals to something else. Shaky hands and bubbling entrails. I remembered staring into the endless void of summers apart and wishing we could turn back time. The autumnal reunions, soft like cashmere. She had a sweetness for my mother and protective streak for young Faithy. We cut class senior year to hold each other for morning moments. So many warm glimpses created by her character and kindness.

The intimacy we developed was just that—intimate. Not collective. I fell for Willow not because she was white, but because she was Willow. I doubt very seriously the role that *choosing* played. But to the extent it did at all, the choice was for a specific human being. A near perfect human being. Willow Carter—one for whom even the slightest alteration would've been a smudge. And she chose me! For reasons all mine—my gifts and my faults—which she accepted and enhanced.

I know the criticisms well, but my time with Willow demands I believe it possible for a Black boy to become enraptured with someone non-Black. Innocently and completely. And that in the midst of that fall, it is possible that he maintains as fiercely as anyone anywhere the magnificence of Black women. My time with Willow pushes me to accept that there are universal human properties, love being first among equals. And then that I ask, *is that really so bad?*

I imagine there are some who think *yes nigga, that's really so bad.* Fair enough. Agree to disagree.

———

It took a long while after Willow to firm my footing. In fact, I'm not sure I ever have. In her immediate wake, however, as I drove two hours south and crammed my belongings into a Georgetown dorm, I was all insecurity. The febrile romance she and I shared cooled—we both had some discovering of our own to do—and as fate would have it, while my first Great floated on, Great #2 braced for impact. When I was leaving Philly, Cara Simmons was moving in, living with a mutual friend who introduced the two of us. We met for the first time while she was on a visit to DC, though her roommate had long primed us both by then. I fell smitten that very night. Cara was gorgeous—freckle-faced, hazel-eyed, and Black. Yes, Black! Jamaican to be exact, but a member of the Uptown subgroup of that ilk which "real Jamaicans" everywhere scoffed at. I could relate.

Cara was my first foray into courtship. Willow and I had known each other our whole lives; any amount of charm she assigned me was as much assumed as it was experienced. Cara made me work for her approval. I saved all week to take her to fancy restaurants we had no business eating in. I scoured the Internet for recommendations that I would then pass off as my own, *Oh this place? I come here all the time! You have to try the barramundi.* I still don't know what a barramundi is, but if she saw through the guise, she was kind enough to produce one of her own. Sporadic messages evolved to spontaneous calls, which blossomed into scheduled FaceTimes—modern romance, I suppose. Before long we were alternating cities. I'd hop the Amtrak to her one Thursday evening, and she'd return the favor the next.

The rhythmic back-and-forth in those days was blissful. Mama and Faith had moved to Manhattan that semester, abandoning the house in Philly. Cara and I treated it as our private palace. I sped to her dorm when I hit town—a whisking-away of sorts. We embraced like it'd been more than days and joked and gossiped on the highway home—who was smooching who, and which girls the sororities were after. I controlled the AUX chord, queueing songs I hoped she'd ask about. My dancehall selection was dated:

They're throwbacks, Cara.
No, they're just old, Cole.

Chestnut Hill was a safe space for us to play house and make-believe. We stayed up on On Demand then chased each other around the place. I toured her through my old haunts. She gave my nostalgia room to breathe. I was still guarded, still playing it cool, but one of those nights, drunk on Bacardi, she got to me. I laid in her arms and grew weepy over family, Dad, and gloomier times. The next morning, we got croissants.

Despite my best efforts, I fell again.

There was something so grown-up about Cara, though she was petite and young-faced. She attended one of those storied boarding schools and understood a world I was just peeking into. In February, we met her old friends and my new ones in New York for the weekend. I spent hours with her, gallivanting between the new and unfamiliar. I was fresh from Philly; dinner and a night out still meant pizza and 40 ozs, not oysters and aperitifs. The group smiled and laughed in unison. It was all so . . . what's the word? . . . civilized. She grazed my fingertips under the table to let me know she was still there.

The next day, I asked her to a hotel in Midtown to meet Mama and her friends for lunch. It wasn't the *hallelujah, praise Jesus!* moment I'd anticipated, but they approved. All the guys did as well—Devon was her biggest fan. There was so much less explaining to do. The space that interracial dynamics had occupied was left void, freeing up acres for that which actually mattered. When she left the table, there were no whispery justifications to concoct nor suggestive glances to parry. All looked right.

There was just one problem: Cara and I argued. We argued big and loud. We're both opinionated people, though the divisions ran deeper than that. She had insecurities to match my own. I kept my guard up, then barked back when she chipped away at it. We've always talked past each other. I was also, if we're being honest, a fuckboy. As a result, we'd regularly huff and puff, then reconcile, only to run it back once more. I hated it. I didn't know how to mix closeness with disagreement—especially full-on hot-blooded disagreement. I was wildly immature, and both of us were stubborn. I grew distant, which only agitated her and in turn, me, more. When May came, she was set to fly back to Kingston for the summer, which was as natural a breaking point as there would be. We left things with an ellipsis and she boarded a plane. Even for all of its outward perfections, that very right situation came to a resolute, if impermanent, end.

If you've been keeping count, Cara makes two. There is, of course, one more Great to discuss—a fitting crescendo, if ever one has existed.

The last was a classmate at Georgetown—a Manhattanite, absent the air of pretension that clung to so many of her Upper West Side compatriots. Her predecessors were thinkers rather than bankers, a trait that proved hereditary. Her name was Anna Ricci, blonde and slender with the two most striking cerulean eyes you'd ever hope to see.[15] She was Italian, as the name suggests, but not like every Joe, Jim, and Johnny from South Philly.

---

15   In truth, I know cerulean only as a word in a thesaurus, but *blue* just don't cut it.

She was real Italian—near enough to the boot that she could still refer to home with a tinge of authentic ambiguity.

She had a boyfriend when we met, a boyfriend who myself and all the other Georgetown boys didn't know, yet were acutely aware of, in much the same way that we were acutely aware of his demotion to irrelevance some months later. She was as eligible a bachelorette as this universe had to offer, but for whatever reason, on one sticky evening in August, she chose me.

Things heated up quickly. After August, there were other nights. There were nights in September and November, and there were nights in March, May, and July as well. Anna registered at just the right dimensions to fit snugly under my arm with her cheek pancaked to my chest, and it was from that position and on those nights that she delicately enlightened me to the boundless expanse of my own ignorance. She was a feminist—loud and proud—and showed no deference to the antiquated notions I unwittingly saddled. I was lost, hopelessly so. I exhaled shame and gulped bewitching wonder.

Yes, for a third time, I fell.

But this time was different. I always maintained a certain casualness with Anna. I feared what it might mean for me to be with a white girl . . . again. I feared the indictments that would follow. As a result, she was never among the welcome committee for Ma's many visits to campus. And on nights that called for libation, she and I met at the pregame rather than dining before and arriving together like all the *real* couples. It couldn't last. The Talk was impending. Yet, even with ample time to prepare, it caught me off guard. It came in late winter, the same way ambushes always do in the movies, with a somber grin, a shot of whiskey, and an invitation outside.

What are we doing?

Fuck. Fuckfuckfuck. My breath escaped, and clear thoughts followed it away.

I wanted to tell her she was smart, but not in a bookish way, though I'm sure she was that too. She was smart in a way that you could just tell she was thinking, pondering even, at times when she wasn't required to, about topics that did not demand for her attention, yet she lent it anyway. And she stood for something. And she wasn't afraid to tell people that she stood for something. And she was kind—deeply kind—but not sweet, and never sugarcoated. And she was sexy. And she was beautiful. Did I mention she was beautiful? And when she looked at me with those stormy, cerulean eyes, I could see my reflection in their polished marble. And we had dimension-bending sex. And one time when I was with another, I shut my eyes tight and longed for her touch, but either my imagination or my experience was too poor a substitute to be mentioned in the same breath as her. And that I did not deserve her—not in the slightest—but I would hold on as long as she'd allow me.

Instead, I was briefer:

I think we should stop this.

Oh.

Yeah.

Is it because I'm white?

No. No, of course not.

Yes. Yes, of course, it was. And she knew me well enough to ask the question. She was all of those marvelous things, but she was also white. Not unpalatably so—not country music and conservativism white, more of a fair-trade coffee, Bohemian variety—but white nonetheless. It was a disqualifying characteristic. Two white girlfriends in only a few years of dating life? People have had their Black cards revoked for less. I couldn't do it. I wasn't ready to hear the censorious twittering again—not from my parents, and certainly not from my boys—so I chose the path of least resistance.

All in all, we spent one calendar year together—one wonderfully warm and deeply intimate year at that—existing the entire time in that odd, undefined relational purgatory which I'm told people of my generation tend to inhabit. Then she boarded a transatlantic flight to spend her semester abroad and we returned to our separate lives.

Breathlessness followed. She'd barely deplaned at her destination before I understood the mistake I'd made. As the August air turned crisp and then cutting, I stuffed fists into pockets on lengthy walks home to combat every urge within me screaming to call, text, or make any sudden movement for her attention. My innards lurched each time my phone chirped, only to most often settle back down to disappointment. It was like life inside a snow globe, never fully at ease when the smallest reminder of her presence could shake the earth and send shit flying. It was a torturous, awakening time.

She returned the following spring, and our months apart had brought about a shift inside me. I still feared the burden of my Blackness in a world where she and I might be together. But the misery without her proved a far worse fate than the petty judgements that would arise by her side. It was my turn to propose a talk and this time, I was ready. I was going to *Casablanca* the shit out of this one. I'd boombox Frank Ocean songs outside her dorm room until the trees swayed to the rhythm and induce a reunion so epic the Greeks would request a do-over.

Then she appeared.

Somehow, it went more awfully than the first. I stammered through one slopped-together soliloquy. Then another. Then another after that. Exasperated, my attempt at a loving sermon collapsed into incoherence. She was unmoved.

It turned out that those months apart had given her time for reflection as well. Did I mention she was smart? And at some point, over the course of that reflection, she'd met a guy—a fair-trade coffee, Bohemian guy. Although I didn't ask, I suspected he was one of the Great Ones.

So, that was that.

Rocky Marciano. Sugar Ray Robinson. Joe Louis. *That happens. What are you gonna do? That's the way it goes, you know?*

Please God, let Sonny be wrong.

It is in the early days of rollicking boyhood that the revelation first bursts upon one, all in a day, as it were. I remember well when the shadow swept across me. I was a little thing, away up in the hills of New England, where the dark Housatonic winds between Hoosac and Taghkanic to the sea. In a wee wooden schoolhouse, something put it into the boys' and girls' heads to buy gorgeous visiting-cards—ten cents a package—and exchange. The exchange was merry, till one girl, a tall newcomer, refused my card,—refused it peremptorily, with a glance. Then it dawned upon me with a certain suddenness that I was different from the others; or like, mayhap, in heart and life and longing, but shut out from their world by a vast veil.

—W. E. B. Du Bois

THE REVEAL

FUCK YOU SAY TO me motherfucker?!

I lunged at the boy, closed the distance between us and gripped his chest, scrunching polyester and flesh between clenched fists.

I hurled him to the ground without an answer. I stood above him and then, for the faintest moment, paused. My fury was tainted by fear. In the midst of my blinding rage, I recalled how far I was from all that was familiar. That I was surrounded by potential enemies. I couldn't take them all on and, if things went south, I couldn't be sure whether my new teammates were riding in with the cavalry or cowering on the sidelines.

On the other hand, to stop then would've been to let the boy win. He deserved to feel some portion of the pain he caused.

Fuck it, I thought. I raised my fist.

A clash like ours was the outcome I'd most feared when I set out that afternoon. It was also the one I most expected.

My morning began in the back of a yellow bus. Bouncing around, I felt a nauseous knot balling up in my stomach and squeezed my head out the mechanical windows to avoid the musty air inside. I journeyed with my soccer team to some Delaware Catholic school none of us had ever heard of. It was the fall of my senior year and I was once again the new kid, kinda. I'd returned to CHA to finish up with the guys I'd started with. The school I came back to was a world away from the one I'd fled years prior, just as I was a world away from my former self.

Some of its changes were positive. CHA had merged with Springside, that fanciful, wondrous plot across the road that had once so captivated me. With the merger came a cultural shift away from the antiquated boys' club model in favor of a more inclusive, tech-savvy academy of the future.

Other changes were cause for caution. By the time I returned, our grade had hemorrhaged nearly all the diverse students I'd known. It was an even whiter place now. When I strode timidly to my first preseason practice weeks earlier, the team I found had hardly a familiar face in the crowd. I was two-thirds the Black population (Evan Wilson was half-Black and held me down with the rest of the representation). Early on, these new teammates greeted me with suspicion, but sweltering days bonded us. By the bus ride, we'd gelled, though much in them still felt foreign to me.

That distance and a growing focus on the game ahead kept me silent for the ride to Delaware. Having arrived, I stepped off the bus and onto gorgeous, spongey fields. Fans crowded onto the grassy knoll above the pitch, dozens more than the group that gathered for our home games. And among the myriad spectators, only two Black faces—Evan's dad and my mama. Add them to the Black players across both teams and you'd get a whopping four Black people at this event. I jogged and stretched as though unbothered, though an anxious vulnerability washed over me while surveying the sea of strange faces. I forced it out of mind. With the sound of the starting whistle, I was ready to compete.

A bloodbath followed. Their side wasn't skilled, but what they lacked in technique they made up for in brutish aggression. The game happened on the grass but also in the air—elbows jabbing jaws and ribs, fists to throats and unspeakable areas, all just beyond the referee's sightline. Nonetheless, our squad stayed the course and, as the final minutes crawled on, we limped to victory.

With seconds remaining, I intercepted a lofted cross in our half of the field and launched the ball to Evan at the opposing 18-yard line. He settled it on his chest, turned, and pitter-pattered on with sharp, punchy steps. A defender tracked him the whole way and, just before reaching the end line, gripped Evan by his sides, lifted him skyward, and launched him off the pitch in a swift maneuver out of fight night. Evan rolled before recovering. I hollered, *Get the hell off my player! Ref, call something!* Upon hearing me, the attacker nearest me perked up. He whipped around, locked his eyes with mine, and spat out, *Fuck you gonna do about it? You shouldn't even be here, nigger.*

Then he let out a deep snort and launched a wad of mucus that cut through the air and splashed on my uniform.

He lit the fuse. I exploded. The potential consequences swirling 'round me weren't enough to contain my eruption. Next I knew, he was on the ground, and I stood above, determined to pummel this stranger to grimy meal.

I reached back, then felt an arm around mine before I swung forth. The moment of hesitation had given Evan time to pick himself up and dart across the field. He was upon me now, pinning elbows to my sides, shouting for me to calm down. As I struggled, two other teammates rushed over and helped him pull me away. I wriggled and griped but was rendered immobile. Finally the ref arrived, whistle blowing furiously. A red card for that asshole. And once he was far enough on his way that the fight wouldn't reignite, another for me. *What*!? As I stormed off, my coach called from the sideline:

Look at me Cole. Don't even look over there. Keep your eyes on me.

I couldn't resist. I glared over mid-stride, just in time to glimpse the maddening grin eating away at his face. He swaggered toward his supporters on the sideline, a gladiator returning for the spoils he'd earned. He turned and blew a kiss my way. A burst of laughter and his cheering section heckled me from the stands.

In the weeks that followed, I often reflected on how I would've reacted if I'd maintained my composure in that moment. I considered the fortitude I'd have shown had I turned and called to them, *Ignorance is hereditary. You've poisoned your children!* Fortitude I wish I possessed. Instead, I raised my middle finger and cast a *fuck y'all too!* over my shoulder without glancing their way.

Why did I react so strongly that day? This was far from the first time I'd encountered ignorance and insults. I'd known ignorance long before traveling to Delaware—the too tough teacher and super circumspect security guard—those who reacted to my race but left me with little more than intuition as evidence. I'd encountered more direct manifestations before as well. In fact, even that precise situation was familiar—it wasn't the first time *nigger* had been flung my way on the pitch. Yet, never had I plummeted into frenzied hysteria the way I did that day.

So, no, the ignorance wasn't it. At least it wasn't the all of it. It was the pride of this boy, soon man, that sent me tumbling; the thick lacquer of brazenness that dripped from his still fresh outburst. His unflinching gaze made epithet seem like observation. My pain drew no empathy, it only inflated him; he jaunted off to the sideline with joy. It was his pride, his eagerness, and the echo of it from the bleachers, that left me disoriented. I knew ignorance before Delaware, but not bigotry. Before Delaware, bigotry was hypothetical for me; it was conceptual and impersonal. That boy, soon man, gave it a face and a name. He converted theory to hard-to-face reality in a single instant, once and for all stripping away the enchanting illusion of my own equality.

That moment has a name in storybooks and film: the reveal. The reveal halts the plotline, diverting the narrative trajectory with a detail so definitional, all else before and after must be reconsidered in its light.

Delaware was my reveal.

I had clung to warm naivete long enough that it had become as much my own as blood and bone. That boy, soon man, snatched it away so definitely he left me flailing, gasping for air. After him, everything had to be reexamined.

It's important to underscore how seemingly insignificant the reveal could've been without context. By any measure, the soccer game was not nearly as dire as the episode at Erin's house party, pressed to the carpet with police gun barrels overhead. But it held indelible impact. Even minuscule moments can pack a monumental punch, forcing you to realign your worldview.

There's something quintessentially token about the experience of abrupt disillusionment. Raised in a coddling environment, repeatedly assured of our exceptionalism, whimsical notions of universal justice become us. For those not so coddled, inequity seeps in day by day. Its lessons are learned gradually, in ways both big and small. The reveal is a more sudden thing, a tidal wave of understanding. It is a bone-crackling crunch, proclaiming loudly that discrimination does not discriminate.

————

In the Fall of 2008, Veronica Graves was a rail-thin high schooler with a wide grin that swallowed half her face when it spread, sending her cheeks to ball up high on their perch. She had these great big, cushy eyes and high-arching eyebrows that said more than words—you needn't have met her mother to know where she got them from. With time, those eyes would harden, and she would grow into her more gangly features to become the striking young woman I met years later. But as a young-for-her-grade ninth grader, Mother Nature and Father Time had yet to do their dance.

Soon after she'd started freshman year, Veronica spotted her first high school Halloween shining gloriously ahead. Lizzie, a close friend, had invited her and others over to her house to kick off the night's festivities. Veronica debated which costume to wear in the lead up, then rushed her mother out the door and into the car when the evening arrived. She refused to be late.

On Lizzie's doorstep for the first time, Veronica peered through the wavy glass for a glimpse of the other side. There were larger figures in there than she'd expected. Her mother waited in the car for her to enter. Neither knew grown-ups had made the guest list.

Lizzie's mom came to greet her, *Veronica dear, so glad you could make it. The girls are in the other room if you'd like to go in and join them.* Veronica responded with a smile and nod but sidestepped the woman to find a crowded room in her path. She started with strides, then timid treads, and finally quickened feet. The room parted and encircled her as she waded across, and she felt the weight of the glares upon her. *They were all staring at me as if I was a problem.* They muttered as adults often do when they presume they can't be heard:

Who's that?

Which one's that?

When'd she become their friend?

Does she live around here?

I've never seen her before . . .

She did hear them, of course but couldn't shrink herself away from the spotlight of attention. She thought it would end once she joined the other girls, but there too she found herself an outsider. *I was with some of my best friends, but I felt like a stranger. It just didn't feel like I should be there even though it was where I was supposed to be, y'know, as far as the plans that we made and everything.* The others joked and fawned and exchanged the occasional knowing glance. Veronica quieted. In a way, she'd never left the stoop, still peering at them through wavy glass. *I wasn't fully myself again until we left the house later that night and we were away from all that.*

Lizzie's house wasn't the first time Veronica had perceived her difference. That came much earlier in life, an incident she recalls just as well. First grade, her first day riding the bus home from school. She gossiped with the other bus riders, six year olds like her, about some of the poor, immature souls still having to carpool with their parents. A boy chimed in, *Oh, you mean the nigger kid?*

Veronica didn't speak. She couldn't. She didn't understand the word then, not fully, but she knew of its power. It was the only just provocation her parents had given her. She could hit this boy now. She *should* hit this boy now. She felt confusion and fear. And most of all, a growing shame. Why hadn't she struck him? She cried all the way home.

That encounter had impact, but there was not yet enough knowledge in Veronica for it to feed on. It didn't smack her with the full weight of her race. Her feelings receded with time, tucked themselves away. Until that Halloween at Lizzie's when they rushed back with newfound force. Along with new feelings: claustrophobia, betrayal. She was older then and though still blindsided by the moment, she knew to call this thing that stung her *prejudice*.

I didn't have to be called a nigger; I felt like one.

―――――

Amira Rasool felt her reveal even later in life, but it arrived with characteristic unsettling force. South Orange, the New Jersey neighborhood she was raised in minutes away from her comedian cousins, is home to many of the tokens I've known throughout my life. It is an apt setting, brimming with eclectically constructed homes that one enters through the *foy-yay*. It's within arm's reach of all the markers of East Coast high society.

Amira was brought up there, but as she would be quick to remind you, that village did not create her. Amira could've stridden out from an A Tribe Called Quest music video, her vibrant, vintage wardrobe reminiscent of an era of Afrocentricity that she missed by the width of just one of her bouncing curls. She's outspoken and unyielding; if the revolution *were* to be televised, Amira would lead network coverage.

She'd moved through both high school and college before the reveal caught up to her. As modern-day rebels do, she migrated to Brooklyn and joined the ranks at a small fashion magazine. She adored the publication and the experience it offered, adding to her portfolio and upping her journalistic chops. Amira had been on staff for a few months when a new hire was brought onto the team and instructed to collaborate with Amira on projects. The two were cordial enough, if not outright friendly, but one dreary day in the office hallways, only one week after the girl joined, Amira overheard her complaining to their editor:

I don't know about Amira. I just really can't stand her attitude.

That lit a firecracker that popped off in Amira's ear. What inspired this opinion of hers? They had shared only the barest of interactions in the week since the new hire joined the team, yet Amira's new coworker had made a judgement with such certainty that she was happy to report it to their superior.

But it was more than a judgement. It was a label. The coworker's language struck a chord. *Attitude*, a word Amira had heard so often through childhood. There was the time she left class and went to the bathroom without permission. She got suspended, on account of her *attitude*. Once, a school security guard claimed Amira called her a bitch. Despite Amira's denial, and without asking any of the witnesses, the administration suspended her. Again, her *attitude* was the problem. By graduation, she'd racked up four or five *attitude* infractions.

Up 'til this moment, Amira never paused to consider what it all meant. She'd long grown disenchanted with high school; she plowed through and delivered herself from its grip. But here was that charge again, years after she had put high school behind her. The new girl's whispered indictment forced Amira to grapple with how her actions were perceived—indeed how they'd always been perceived—and how her hallmark confidence and strength would always be judged through the prism of her Blackness.

In Amira's case, as in Veronica's, subtleties illuminated an entire side of reality that she had yet to fully reconcile. For them both, the reveal recalled memories from far and near, reopening interactions they'd long filed away. It popped a fantasy narrative they'd inflated. Their reveals were made doubly impactful because of those tiny pointers that had so long gone ignored. It forced them to reconsider all those myriad interactions in a new light. In a film, the storyline ends soon after enlightenment; the character can never go back to comfortable ignorance. They are changed forever.

In real life it's not so clear cut.

Though we tokens might understand, for the first time, bigotry's might, the fantasy would come calling us again. Privilege, and Not Really Black, and *oh, I don't usually like Black people, but I like you*—would breathe their siren song again. Months, years without confrontation would work to lull us back into blissful ignorance.

But should we fall, we do not fall to our starting point. Reality cannot be unseen. We know what to look for now, so even minute transgressions trigger reminders of the harshness of the reveal. And in the America that I have come to know, reminders of our insignificance in the eyes of those who construct their own superiority exist everywhere.

———

When the news broke that Darren Wilson would not be indicted,

I was on shift. Mama had long spun tales of working her way through college, walking uphill both ways to get to class. Freshman year, I thought it time I author one of my own. A new bar had just opened on Georgetown's campus and I was hired to be its first bouncer—an insult to proud, *real* bouncers everywhere. The place was so remarkably uncool that there was no bouncing to be done. And even if there had been, my frail frame would've been of little use. Instead, I was tasked with patronizing parents and professors each night, insisting they produce ID—we were on a college campus after all; one can never be too careful.

From my post at the door of the Bulldog Tavern, I watched the grand jury's non-indictment decision roll in and jolted out of the repetitive hush of pseudo-bouncing. Ferguson had a dark, discriminatory history of policing—logic should've prepared me for the announcement—still it landed with a crunch. It reminded me of the soccer field a year prior. It reminded me of bigotry's bigness. It reminded me of my smallness. There at my job, still hand-to-handing IDs, something imploded within and left me a smoldering, open crater.

My phone pinged, and I looked down to see a text from Sam Agre, a close friend from my time at Penn Charter, and quite possibly the most down white man on this planet:[16]

I can't imagine how you must be feeling right now, but just know I'm blown away too. I looked it up and if we left tonight, we could make it to Ferguson by morning. You want to go?

I was conflicted. The counterargument was clear: I had

---

16   Honorable mentions: Eminem, Bernie Sanders, and Tommy from *Power*.

teetered to the end of a long shift after an even longer day of classes and, no matter the emotions that swelled within, the thought of twelve wakeful hours behind the wheel of Agre's Camry sent a shudder down my spine. But Mama's tales of university spoke of the other side of this argument. She was in Berkeley back when Berkeley was *Berkeley*. Angela Davis was *Professor* Angela Davis to her. Her voice in my head reminded me of the difference the young could make, should make, while the flame inside still burned strong.

For the first time, I felt her example pulling me into action. I had a duty to struggle in those streets with the masses of men and women who looked like me, pressed under the thumb of injustice. So, I texted a cousin in St. Louis to make sure we had a place to stay the night, and then I responded to Agre:

I get off in a couple hours. Let me run back to my dorm to throw some clothes in a bag, but then I'm in.

My shift ended, and I clocked out. I slipped out of the tavern then broke into a sprint and didn't stop running until I reached my dorm. The protests had intensified since Agre first texted me. My passion climbed with them. I had to be there.

In retrospect, I can identify the droplets of protest-tourism–inspired adrenaline coursing through my veins. There were moments that felt like peering out the door of the plane just before leaping. But that was not all of it, not even the majority. For I also remember sensing that we, the collective "we," were on the cusp of something significant. I'd followed our activism in the time since Trayvon was felled. Watching those bodies pour into the street, chanting in unison, mourning the way humans mourn, they seemed a crucial, unignorable, mass. I belonged in their ranks.

I was all packed and waiting in my dorm's common room when I received the next text from Agre:

I just talked to my Pops and he said they shooting out there bro. I'm out.

And just like that, he yanked me back from the edge.

I considered my response. As I did, my hallmates filed into the common room, crowding on the couches around me for a view of the TV. They treaded lightly at first, sensing my delicate composure, but boldened quickly. The room livened, and discussion swirled. I heard their conservative commentary and two-bit name game. They watched the same screen I did yet seemed to invert the images it showed. I saw mourners; they saw instigators. I saw overwhelming grief; their plotline led to rampage. *Thugs*, they said.

Those streets had seen more than their share of injustice over the years. Months earlier, a man had taken his last breath while face down on them, his corpse left to rot for hours. And today, the man who snatched the vitality from his chest, made a body out of somebody, sighed in relief. And all these kids could talk about was broken windows. I felt their gaze and it burned hot on my skin. I steamed. I had to get out of there. I texted Agre again:

Come pick me up bro. Let's go to the White House.

Sam's Camry wove around the restless bodies crowding the streets. He got us as close as he could then parked the car, and we walked the rest of the way. The throngs thickened as we neared. There was a heaviness—so many dark faces in dark draping behind a black sky. As we reached the epicenter, the mood became more uncertain, seemingly vacillating between depression and exultation. Sadness and anger were prominent—the air was pungent with them. Strangers grieved and embraced and gritted teeth and bundled fists. Emotion wed them to Ferguson, and something along the way had been severed.

But underneath the grief simmered a joy that fought to surface as we progressed. Everyone there was brother or sister to everyone else there, coming together after a lifetime apart. We'd assembled for a family reunion. Despite the circumstances, few could look to that sea of young, Black people, participating in structures established for their belittlement, and not smile. The seesawing emotions caused conflict—how to voice anger without hate, grief without hopelessness, all while suppressing the excitement of the moment.

We marched through the streets and recited the chants that would soon become slogans, but it was not the dramatic marathon I'd expected. The crowds dissipated a few hours after they'd congregated. Sam and I stuck around a bit longer, but by midnight, the litter strewn about were the only remnants of our march, so we walked back to his car and drove home.

A collective catharsis claimed the streets of Washington that night but not in the way I had hoped for or expected. Hundreds were out there; the most vocal contingent were students from Howard University. We felt powerful, moving as a single organism, pressing our government to make good on its promise. We knew the promises past, broken, and deferred, just as we knew the mantle we'd inherited. I sought to honor that tradition. But when all was said and done, it felt like a bad costume party. I dragged volatile emotions with me to the protest, but when it ended just before midnight, the satisfaction I'd exchanged them for was unearned. The action was a fleeting antidote to my helplessness. I spent the rest of the week spying Ferguson from the comfort of my common room couch. And though perhaps my capacity for empathy was greater than that of my hallmates, my impact on the outcome was identical. I was ashamed at the redemption I'd claimed for myself by dressing up as revolutionary; and even more ashamed that I'd so soon settled back to bystander.

Years later, the emotional tumult of that night is a vivid memory. It induced a reveal-like vulnerability—a disconcerting nakedness to the elements that was primal. The announcement of Wilson's escape from consequence speared the soul, brutally reminding me of my positionality in this world. It was a reminder so harsh in its severity, I assumed it must have been felt by all. I was wrong.

Amira crystallized the sentiment perfectly:

I don't actually think I remember where I was [when the decision came out], but I think that's also a result of me being immune to this stuff at this point. Maybe a few years ago I would've remembered but seeing as how this happens all the time now, I think they've all kind of blurred into one experience and I always get the same feeling each time it happens now.

She was right. That night remains with me because of the injustice it unveiled, but also because of its novelty—the novelty of petitioning our government and bartering helplessness for action. Had I not, it may very well have receded and diffused to the incoherent din of despondency I've assigned the whole cast of African Americans who have met unjust ends, just as it did for Amira.

————

Reflecting on the fates of Michael Brown, Trayvon Martin, Sandra Bland, Jordan Davis, Tanisha Anderson, Eric Garner, Laquan McDonald, Tamir Rice, Walter Scott, Freddie Gray, Ezell Ford, Alton Sterling, Dontre Hamilton, John Crawford III, Dante Parker, Akai Gurley, and the countless before and since, every token I spoke to felt pain. But none of those events had the deeply personal impact that I'd anticipated. Very few told me that these high-profile deaths swayed their sense of security or the perceived safety of their loved ones.

But there was a much less notorious case that had a disproportionately massive impact on all the tokens I spoke with and crossed the threshold from upsetting to endangering.

The victim in this case, then twenty-year-old Martese Johnson, wrote about his experience in an article that appeared on *Vanity Fair*'s website some months after the assault.

The night of March 18, 2015, three white Alcoholic Beverage Control officers asked me for identification outside of a bar adjacent to the University of Virginia's grounds. I showed them my I.D., which they wrongly assumed was a fake I.D. After a brief interaction with these officers, I was slammed to the ground violently, detained with handcuffs and leg shackles, and arrested without justification. As the officers pinned me to the ground with their knees, blood flowed freely from my face and my friends and classmates surrounded the scene, screaming with indignation and anger. They watched helplessly as I yelled, "How did this happen? I go to U.Va.!" When I was picked up and dragged away by these officers, glimpses of my ancestors' history flashed before my eyes. Although it could never compare to a life of slavery, for those hours, I had no freedom, no autonomy, and no say in what was happening to me. I cried for a long time that night—not because of my physical wounds (though there were many) or possible jail time (I was charged with two misdemeanors that were eventually dropped), but because my lifelong vision of sanctuary in success was destroyed in seconds.

Video of the altercation went viral. Martese yells, *I go to UVA you fucking racists!* while pinned to the pavement, arms twisted and cuffed behind his back, his face barely recognizable with glistening, red tributaries zigzagging here and there. All the tokens I know are disturbed by the broad canon of Black brutalization, but the Martese fiasco was of a different order than the others.

Jackson, who first brought this story to my attention, thought the difference a question of relevance. The fates of the others were tragedies, but distance rendered them foreign and somewhat generic. Not unlike the impersonal cloud of tragedy that, for Americans, hovers above my ancestral home,

Ethiopia—images of ashy children with cleft lips and hotlines to dial. Their suffering can be felt deeply. It can trigger sorrow, empathy even. But never fear. Watching those other cases play out, our different worlds meant that we didn't feel that same primal fear. *I was less afraid for my life because I knew I wouldn't move in those spaces. In the spaces where I am, I'm around enough white people that a cop isn't going to do that to me.*

That was until Jackson watched a UVA honor student pour blood onto concrete. *That is the moment when I was like "I am not safe."*

Not even in the world of privilege and of Not Really Black.

Martese's misfortune thundered into Veronica's world as she sat in a George Washington University classroom on an otherwise lackadaisical Thursday afternoon. A text from a friend diverted her attention from the lecture:

Something's happened with Martese. He got beat up by the cops.

She sat, confounded. She considered herself a friend to Martese but not a very close one. Why was he telling her this? Then the friend sent along pictures of Martese, pictures he had taken in the middle of the beating the night before. Those pictures, much like the ones that would soon spread across media outlets, showed Martese's brown skin nearly invisible, hidden behind a mask—slick and cherry red. Veronica's heart sank. Butterflies flapped in her stomach and chest, then perched in the impossible-to-reach crypt in the back of her throat. She broke down. Right there at her desk, in the middle of class, she sobbed.

It's obvious why the Martese episode bothered them so. He

was one of us. He was bloodied on sacred soil, a site where the famous mononyms first wove America's mythology. When earth shakes beneath the Harvards of the South, tremors are felt in the Harvards of the North. The legacy of prideful self-affirmation in those bubbles make it easy to believe *I'm around enough white people that a cop isn't going to do that to me.* Whimsical notions of invincibility can't last forever though. The blows that landed on Martese rocked many others. In the end, the respectability politics we had unwittingly pulled tight around our shoulders proved to be more blindfold than bulwark.

But can it be that simple? Consider the fallen: Tamir was twelve. John Crawford was shopping. Tamir was twelve. Jordan Davis liked rap. Trayvon Martin was in a gated community. Renisha McBride needed help. Tamir was twelve. The sheer randomness of their unnatural ends seems a boast on the measure of Death's wingspan, that it can reach out and touch us at will. But somehow this relentless accumulation of tragedy diminishes our anger and fear, instead of compounding it. Why?

I'm reminded of a shameful impulse that rushed me on the occasion of Michael Brown's slaying, days after our rumblings in the District:

If only it were me.

The longing first entrenched itself inside me with the surveillance video of Michael shoving a store clerk shortly before his death. The outlets played it on loop. Over and over and over, as if it were relevant. As if it were a capital crime. As if it justified the putrid scent wafting from his skull, made porous and left to sizzle in the Missouri sun. And each time they showed those images, I heard a hushed whisper in my mind—if only it were *my* last breaths still floating in that thick summer air. *Then* the world would learn. Then the politicians would mourn Black loss and even Fox News would proclaim injustice for another Black boy perished. Mommy and Daddy know people. And those people know people. They'd make it so. *Plus, I am a Georgetown student,* I thought. My move to prestige coupled my fate with those white folks; I carried their name. My annihilation spelled out mutually assured destruction. There would be outrage! My life has value. It must—even in the eyes of those that stripped Michael Brown of his.

It wasn't logic I heard. It was hubris. And the lure of martyrdom. And the privilege of growing up in circumstances that have exclaimed my *difference.* And the facile impulse to embrace that *difference.* And my defense mechanisms ringing; ensuring that self-deception in order to shield me from what our likeness would entail. That I am as vulnerable as he was.

The Martese Johnson incident is a tale of dual tragedy. There is the original offense: excessive and undeserved force unleashed on yet another Black body. But there is also the tragedy of white legacy being needed to enhance the value of Black life. Every headline about Martese's beating took the same form; *Black UVA student. . . .* Just as the headlines about Trayvon and Tamir and Jordan mentioned black hoodies and toy guns and loud music. The mentions of UVA in connection with Martese were intended to communicate certain truths about Martese's aspirations and potential, his disposition and guiltlessness. Ultimately, his worth.

I'm sure those assumptions were largely true. I have met Martese in the years since and he struck me as supremely generous and congenial, the same way I'd describe my closest friends and how I hope they'd describe me. His trials were a particularly heartrending reveal precisely because so many of us saw ourselves in him. But I feel a sadness wash over me when considering why the many incidents before his did not pack the same proverbial punch.

My use of *the reveal* as neologism was an act of theft, stolen from Du Bois's description of his *revelation*. Du Bois was born to mixed-race Northerners in the still frothy wake of the Civil War. His childhood was spent in a Euro-American town in Massachusetts where he attended an integrated school with predominately white classmates before graduating to Fisk University for his bachelor's degree. He'd, of course, go on to receive a PhD from Harvard (the first of our kind to do so), cofound the NAACP, and live out a successful career as both an intellectual and activist (before falling out of favor with the US government, joining the communist party, and taking his last breaths on African soil). Du Bois was a token.

His description of the reveal, authored over a century ago, encapsulates the crucial elements of this experience that still make it particular to tokens today. Both the seeming banality of a young girl refusing his valentine and the *suddenness* of the realization it caused are part and parcel to the disruptive impact of the reveal. So too is the reckoning of a *vast veil*. That veil, intangible and insurmountable, separated him from his white peers who, through privilege alone, operated without fear of prejudice.

But Du Bois only got it half right. The reveal does birth the reckoning of a veil between tokens and the white world we inhabit. But as one veil is constructed, or more accurately, epiphanized, another is dismantled. When we run up against that which separates us from the white world, we see also that which connects us as Black people. We are provided a glimpse beyond a veil that has long existed between us and our counterparts for whom injustice is a familiar force.

Tokens develop in a segment of society that is unconstrained by the markers of second-class citizenship. We are sheltered from the overt manifestations of structural racism—the most unjust elements that largely define the Black plight are foreign to us—thus we are saved the burden of confronting our difference. Our environment is one of opportunity and we are molded into both products and pursuers of that opportunity. Our aspirations in youth are constrained by our imaginations alone, and these imaginations float freely over long stares from parents and around attitude-inspired suspensions. The reveal occurs only when these fanciful ideals collide head-on with the jarring reality beyond the veil that privilege has erected, a reality that our counterparts in less forgiving environments have been socialized into since birth.

THE BIG REVEAL

HEY FAITHY WHAT'S GOOD?

What the hell is going on, dude?

Chill. We still have plenty of ways to win this.

But Cole. . . .

Faith, just stop. He won't win. Go to sleep. I'll talk to you in the morning.

And now I can't summon the courage to call her back. I knew then that I was wrong to be so definite, to sweep her doubt away with condescension, but my role was reassurance; what was I supposed to tell her? I couldn't admit that I felt the looming, ominous presence of our shared future as severely as she, or that I feared more greatly for the safety of her mind and body than my own. I couldn't admit that I shared her alarm; that with each vote counted, it grew increasingly likely that the world she'd greet tomorrow would threaten her more greatly than the one I commanded she steal away from tonight. So, I feigned certainty in a moment when there was precious little to be had. I'm sure also that I so yearned for the words to be true, that it comforted me to hear them spoken, even if by my own voice.

In the days since Trump's victory, a growing group of sages has sprung up, claiming to have foreseen the outcome of this election. I am not one of them. As a Black man in this country, it is almost definitional that I be cynical of the American promise I've been sold. When others speak of this country's supreme goodness, I am meant to scoff, then ask after my forty acres and my mule. I am the reality check; meant to remind white-washers and misrememberers of the many times we as a nation fell short. This campaign season put that cynicism on trial and witnessed its fall to unfounded optimism. Drunk on an American Dream I did not know I held, I peered into my crystal ball and saw the same thing as every pollster and pundit in the country.

And so, as the night unfolds, I become one of many taking a bullet at every battleground:

Florida? No problem we'll still get North Carolina and fight in Ohio.

North Carolina? Tough loss but he can't win without Michigan and Pennsylvania.

Michigan and Pennsylvania? What the fuck is going on. . . .

Nobody is calling the election yet, but slowly, the new reality creeps around the corner of my mind. Hope is a sticky thing, loosening only when scraped away by the inevitable. The process is taxing physically; my limbs turn rubbery and leaded, my chest concave. My thoughts stop coming in logical streams, instead flitting about from worry to screaming worry: my sister!; the environment!; my immigrant family!; my people!; my body. I sense the announcement is near. I need a drink.

Friends had gathered at The Tombs, a bar just off campus, so I throw on a sweatshirt and hurry to meet them. As I walk, a brisk breeze toys with the thin cotton, but I press on without much notice. Soon, I'll be asked my opinion—can I mutter my way into composure before I arrive? But when I push open the door, the typically lively bar is like an abandoned saloon from an old Western; the air pregnant with stale beer and heavy sighs. A projector down the front is still rolling CNN to a room of empty chairs—scattered about or overturned. The place is set for a joy that never arrived. Only a few patrons still dot the scene. Their faces echo Faith's question: *What the hell is going on?*

Kobby and Pat are among the remnants sitting up front; I give my back to the screen to face them. It feels like the only thing that keeps us all from floating away is the decades of sludge sticking us to the floor. We order several pitchers of beer and talk each other dizzy 'til the lights come on for closing time. By now, the result is confirmed.

Pat leans over. *We're going to head down to the White House to see what's happening. You want to come?* No. No, I do not. I want to mourn alone, far away from the bubbling rumbling on Pennsylvania Avenue. I wish them well and head out back into the night alone. The frigid fall air cuts deeper now. I pull a cigarette from my pocket, light it, and take a drag, just to steady my trembling hands.

When I get home I flick on the TV. Van Jones is choking out knee-jerk reactions through tears, fearful of the message this election will send to the youngest Americans. I am drifting into slumber when a rattling vibration jumps me awake. It's Kobby texting me:

You up g?

Yeah.

This crazy. I just went to the White House with Pat and had to leave cus I literally started crying profusely.

Me too. I had to hold back tears while talkin' to Ma on the phone. It's gonna be a shitty four years.

Bro, I've never seen so much open hatred.

Lots of Trump people there?

Majority Hillary but a big loud Trump contingent. Bro it was as if all the racists had just had a big coming out party. Group of white dudes were yelling "fuck your rights." Never thought I'd hear someone say that in the flesh.

This is the America we've always lived in man. Only difference today is that it's voted in and state-sanctioned.

———

I was not on Georgetown's campus on September 12, 2001, but if pressed to imagine it, I'd picture November 9, 2016. I report that without even the slightest hint of hyperbole. The collective decided on despondency. Wednesday and Thursday materialized and evaporated with the wispy ephemerality of a dream. Both brought rock-bottom expectations and quarter-hearted efforts. Conservative pundits spent the week lambasting universities for overindulging in their students' post-election pity parties. They were referring to the Hoyas. There was an implicit, and in some cases, explicit sense of *fuck it* after the election that spread through most of my peers and extended even to the educators, decades our senior. It was as if the collective conscious imagined, *Hey the world's ending anyway, how much could homework really matter?* Over time those thoughts would give way to more pragmatic ones; but for the time being, Georgetown would grieve for the death of an America it had so speciously imagined.

I didn't allow myself the same, drawn-out recoil. Wednesday was my allocated time for despair. By Thursday morning, I woke determined to return for the real life I'd left in a Tombs booth. That evening, tired of the continuing haze, I phoned Jackson for a dose of clarity, hoping he'd reel me back to earth.

He didn't disappoint. For him, the impact was twofold. The first was that Election Day served as *affirmation that our country is still populated by myriad hateful, racist, homophobic, backward, nonprogressive people.* It was a reveal. We both knew these views to exist out there, in the abstract, but Trump's election had them parading down Main Street, USA, flags raised. We thought that decades of struggle forced those beliefs into terminal decline, but they had merely retreated to the shadows to regroup. We no longer needed to peer into the dark to uncover the depth of hate this country harbors, to see just how passionately we, and others, are despised. It was the hate that confronted Kobby in front of the White House. Not all who voted for Donald Trump did so with blackened hearts, but there is a not-so-insignificant minority of voters who did. Election Day revealed to many of us just how ugly the face of bigotry could be and left us astounded that in 2016 it could still find new reasons to smile.

The second of Jackson's disappointments was more nuanced, more relevant too. For, while hatred has shown its newly emboldened face, it will still, I expect and pray, inhabit the *out there*. I won't, in all likelihood, rub up against prejudice's most abrasive agents in the day-to-day (though, you never know). His greater concern was, *those people who voted for Donald Trump who knew his rhetoric was wrong and dangerous, who even acknowledged how deeply wrong it was, and yet determined that the better of two evils was someone who could unrepentantly attack my identity.* Those fellow Americans lie at the root of my anxieties too, those remarkably normal and rational individuals who cordoned off their most basic understandings of injustice. The individuals who said, *Yeah, he said "grab them by the pussy," but . . .* were in some cases the same individuals Jackson and I had grown up with. These old pals and the choices they've made stir an uneasiness that extends beyond disappointment.

Cole, y'know we went to high school in a white context but grew up and were raised in Black communities in the sense that all of our family and close family-friends were Black. At school, we wanted to fit in, wanted to be like everyone else. And it was easier because we had smaller adjustments to make. We had just as much money as everyone else, our moms were in the same clubs, and our day-to-day experiences were the same as theirs. Yet, a consequence of fitting in is that we end up making friends with people who no longer see us as Black.

That was no big deal while I was living in the high school bubble, but then I got to college and my world expanded. It's then that I realized that some of these people don't even know me. They know Jackson the fun lacrosse player, but they don't realize that I am a Black man confronting America.

What happened with this election was that I realized that some people just aren't my friends. How could you call yourself my friend and then vote for a man whose rhetoric is literally the antithesis to my identity? I had to cut them loose. They couldn't even see me. I was an Oreo, their rich Black friend. I wasn't a Black man.

All the token crew I've contacted since the election share the same feeling; struggling with this realization—seeing, for the first time in a long time, how we are seen. Close friends prove most problematic. We see them celebrating and wonder how many other ways we may have misjudged them. We'd grown sedentary in our attachments, surrounded ourselves with the same individuals long enough that we'd divorced the happenings of our bubbles from the broader context they're cooked in. Only a cosmic force like Trump could force us to reassess the friendships we took for granted, which we assumed to be firm.

Just like Jackson was, I found myself pushed to reexamine friendships I had held close since well before I could remember.

————

I stumbled out of Professor Lance's classroom and into the

street, still processing what the hell I'd sat through. It'd been only hours since Trump barreled into the presidency, and Lance's class on nonviolence was like a visit to the crash site. All were there: children of the undocumented, fearful of separation; young victims of sexual assault, feeling the walls closing in; LGBTQ-identifiers, newly panicky and exposed. Lance rerouted the agenda and opened the floor. They all took turns, heaving their concerns over a sniffling chorus. Their fears inflated the place. By the end, many had melded together—a puddle of worry and despair.

I held it together in the classroom, but afterward found myself on the pavement, bent and gasping. My phone chimed. Serena, a close friend from the Chestnut Hill days, had texted. *Hey. I just posted in the high school GroupMe about Trump, which is kinda pointless, but just pissed me off seeing Chris and Henry's posts last night.* I'd averted GroupMe and all other virtual gathering places through the morning and afternoon hours for fear of what I might find. I knew how, left unchecked, conversation there could veer into the insensitive and unwelcomed. But Serena seemed bothered. I told her I'd take a look and back her up if need be.

I logged in to find a few had scribbled fiery Trump slogans across the walls of our chat. They trolled, pointing and laughing, salting our wounds. I was shocked, though in retrospect, not surprised. There had been plenty of talk before the election, and all voices seemed to be speaking in unison. But as we discovered, the MAGA-ites had been lying in wait; now the results gifted them vindication, which they seemed determined to make the most of. Their snobbery, their indignance, their sore-winnery shocked my already tender sensibilities. I penned a storm. The last line read, *Bigotry has become state-sanctioned and bigots everywhere are rejoicing. If you chose Trump on your ballot, they are your brothers in jubilation, whether you choose to acknowledge it or not.* Then I left the chat.

Was I right to suggest that some of my oldest friends were bigots (or at least the *brothers* of bigots)? Perhaps not. I was angry; for my friend Serena, for me, for all of us. But even now, days removed and slightly more levelheaded, I do think there is an irreducible truth about the nature of racism that those longtime friends are yet to understand.

Chris and Henry, like the conservative commentators, treat the word *racist* like taxonomy, as though you could creep through the brush below the Mason-Dixon Line and spot yourself a wild one. For them, racist equals ignorant white trash. For them, unless you are a hootin', tootin', hooded hillbilly for whom the sun rises and sets on racial superiority, you are of a different order; you deserve absolution. You are Not Really Racist.

That, of course, is not how prejudice operates; it is a more insidious, pervasive thing. It is a prevailing set of sentiments in which even they—white people with a Black friend—can participate.

Trump's racism elevated this election from the political realm to the moral. He has shown himself over the past many months, deeming Mexicans rapists and Muslims forbidden. Before that, there was birtherism. Before that there was *laziness is a trait in blacks*, discriminatory housing practices, and *BRING BACK THE DEATH PENALTY. BRING BACK OUR POLICE!* for five innocent boys. The vote wasn't a question of right or left, but of right or wrong (or, if you prefer, wrong and *substantially more wrong*).[17]

His is a brand of prejudice that is puzzling only in its anachronism—its total lack of nuance or remorse. He's reminiscent of a bygone, golden era of white supremacy when Black and brown degradation was public discourse. To the reasonable, *did he really just say that?* is the only response before denouncement.

Electing him will produce consequences that only time will fully reveal. They will not, however, be random, nor entirely unpredictable. I can predict with near certainty that they will not be borne by Chris. Nor by Henry. "Wrong" will fall hard on those bodies that look like mine and harder still, I fear, on the ones like Faith's.

That fear was the source of my anguish and my fury toward my friends. Perhaps they contained cognitive dissonance, or they blinded themselves to the real-world consequences of his rhetoric. Or perhaps, disappointingly, they saw in him a closeted piece of themselves. Each case would be an expression of privilege that is distinctly their own. For when a burden is ultimately placed, it will be added to the backs of those Atlases

---

17   This is all to say nothing of his combative views of women, which are equally well-documented, and concern me at least as much as his dim regard for the many cultures of the world.

already shouldering a deep history of prejudice and neglect in this nation.

I can't yet compartmentalize their political views because I can't yet shake the feeling that those views, wittingly or unwittingly, discount my humanity. Thanks to those kids, who helped empower Trump's ascension, I feel an overwhelming sense of vulnerability for myself, my loved ones, and my people that was absent just days ago.

In this time, I've considered the words of Rabbi Heschel, *that indifference to evil is worse than evil itself, that in a free society, some are guilty, but all are responsible,* and I am reminded that there is no great insight in placing blame where it most logically lies— where indeed it is most welcomed. After finger-pointing must come the mirror. What role did we, the dismayed, play in recent events, and what role are we to play in their remedy? The election bore out the tenuous relationship our country continues to have with the height of its ambitions. That struggle is not an aspect of this nation, but its core. Hard-won liberties are not to be taken for granted. Growing comfortable in progress, developing a belief in its inevitability, is the surest way to usher in its opposite. In these next four years, more than ever, *all are responsible.*

———

In this period of transition and growing social change, there is a dire need for leaders who avoid the extremes of "hotheadedness" and "Uncle Tomism." The urgency of the hour calls for leaders of wise judgment and sound integrity—leaders not in love with money, but in love with justice; leaders not in love with publicity, but in love with humanity; leaders who can subject their particular egos to the greatness of the cause. To paraphrase Holland's words: God give us leaders!

A time like this demands strong minds, great hearts, true faith and ready hands;

Leaders whom the lust of office does not kill;

Leaders whom the spoils of life cannot buy;

Leaders who possess opinions and a will;

Leaders who have honor; leaders who will not lie;

Leaders who can stand before a demagogue and damn his treacherous flatteries without winking

Tall leaders, sun crowned, who live above the fog in public duty and private thinking.

—Martin Luther King, Jr.

What's the world for you if you can't make it up the way you want it?

—Toni Morrison

CLIFTON'S CONGREGATION

TEQUILA AND DALLIANCE KEPT me up 'til dawn. I was still fog-headed when she nudged me at 7:00 a.m. with a phone in my face. *It's your mom, Cole.* I grunted, *Huh?* She thrust it in my hand.

What? What is it?

Son, I'm not sure how to say this—Harry's Dad died last night.

I lumbered out of bed,

What? What're you talking about?

I stumbled on the first step, stiffed the doorframe, and barely caught myself on the second.

Killed himself.

Her words sopped up the liquor, wisped around the room like dandelion poppies.

I need to go. Someone should tell our friends.

199

Still delirious, and more than a little drunk, I spent the next two hours ticking names off a call list.

I did little to blunt the bite, less still with each successive conversation. I was confused myself. Hearing it laid bare, over and over, cleared space in my mind for the truth to nest.

Breezy! How you been, man? What's good?

Harry's Dad. . . .

Yeah?

Shot himself. He's dead.

. . . What?

On the other end, there was disbelief and shock and sorrow. *Call me if you need me* and *I'm here if you want to talk.* Then a dial tone and another round. Ill-informed whispers had reached a few before I could, stories that it was Harry himself who had abandoned this world. Heaves of relief punctuated those conversations, followed by deeper heaves of guilty realization.

I first met Harry at summer camp when we were both still young enough for that to make sense. The camp overtook the campus of a New England college, luring prep school types away from distant nations and nearby neighborhoods. The curriculum offered courses in dark room photography and model rocketry, plus museum excursions to the city's center. I rolled my eyes so often I thought they might stick there. Harry did too. We both thought ourselves athletes; both yearned to break from the decrepit classrooms and tumble across the field at center campus. It drew us near. We stayed in touch through the years; spent the fall messaging about our last summer and the spring, our next. We returned to New England each year on our own terms: soccer training academy, not camp. A week here, two weeks there. He wasn't my closest friend, nor I his, but there's an intimacy to accompanying another through every stage. We were close in that way.

Harry's dad used to drive over an hour to make it for our intramural matches during those soccer summers away. Spotting Mr. Clifton from the field, I often wondered if God was forced to ration masculinity after crafting him. Mr. Clifton's style of spectating was an action verb; his energy cut the sluggish summer heat to grip you. In times of intense competition, he scorned refs then bellowed inspiring quotables from the sidelines. His love for his child was so all-consuming, so spectacalized, I thought Harry might chug it at halftime then ride it 'round the pitch like a magic carpet.

I clambered into the backseat of Mr. Clifton's sedan after the game that first year and for many years thereafter. Our training concluded, I'd stay the night with them and wake the next morning to continue on to Martha's Vineyard. The streets we traveled to their home were foreign, yet intensely familiar. They could have been Chestnut Hill's. Harry pointed to his school as we passed. It splayed across the window greedily, hording acre upon emerald acre for itself. I praised its grandeur, as he hoped I would. The true marvel was that it appeared airlifted from so many of the suburbs I'd known. The ride to his place was drawn-out déjà vu.

To arrive at the Clifton's doorstep was to be overwhelmed

with the hope of what could one day be. Open the door and there they were, five blonded, smiling heads (plus one cherry-tomato-red head), peppy and picturesque, asking after uncles, cousins, and pets I forgot I once had. Their home was adorned with pictures of holiday parties and backyard barbecues and poolside drinks by moonlight. They danced about its floorplan, perfectly in sync to a humming household rhythm only they seemed to hear. There was the occasional hiccup, barking and back-and-forth, but even that too seemed melodious, forgotten nearly as soon as it'd arrived. They made a beautiful Christmas card.

Mr. Clifton's service drew their village out on a June day that stuck like a wet rag. Hundreds descended upon the small chapel—the same chapel where the Cliftons were once wed. They bunched into the pews and across the aisles, then spilled out the back when there wasn't any consecrated ground to be had. Christmas-Easter churchgoers slow-cooking, bowing on cue. I could see them all from my seat in the overflow, behind the altar. They wept. There's often a thin touch of gaiety to funerals—any excuse to bring old friends together. *It was their time*, and *He lived well*, and so on. None there though. Lives deprived decades leave mostly despair behind. Many, many wept.

I didn't join them. Much as I loved Mr. Clifton, and much as my heart ached for Harry, tears did not come to me.

Squished between their world, beholding a community that could've so easily been my own, I found myself strangely detached. I couldn't help but observe. I spotted Ma and Faith to the back-left, an Indian man upfront, to the right, and then there was everyone else, the navy blazers with gilded snaps, the pearls and parted slick-backs. The Clifton's village, faceless almost.

It prompted memories of other rooms and other times where I'd been both present, and not present. An engagement party in a glitzy Manhattan restaurant. Thirty-something waiters in white posted behind thirty-something kosher-only buffet stations, ready to serve. There was a band in one room, a DJ in the other, and hundreds of people hopping between the two. Months later, at the wedding reception for the same couple, the new in-laws dragged me by the collar onto the dance floor where we bounced with the newlyweds to fist-pumping beats.

Or Miami the year prior. Another wedding for the sibling of a Georgetown friend. The reception was set at a ruinous castle by the sea—the century-old mansion of some American oligarch. I showed up in dark jeans and seersucker—I didn't yet know the protocol and looked and felt uncouth. The crowd was bilingual, so I missed much of what there was to laugh about. I wandered the sculpture garden and set my champagne flute down near a cherub's ass. I returned to the group just as nighttime blanketed the grounds and salsa'd 'til daylight drew nigh. It wasn't just beautiful; it belonged in the Louvre.

Weddings and funerals, seminal moments in the lives of their protagonists. The honorees were whittled into personhood by the crowd that assembled to lift them up. Looking out at Mr. Clifton's crowded chapel, I considered that all on this earth that still mattered to the man was likely under that roof. If it could be strung out and glued together, our collective memory would contain the all of him. Or nearly so. Whether in exultation or grief, I find a strange beauty in our ability to open doors on summer days and watch the weight of a person's life stream in two by two. That experience, too, is like the view from above. And from up there, in all three, I was struck by the similarity.

It wasn't a moment of epiphany akin to my Bahamian excursion with the white tourists and reclaimed land. I didn't relapse to imposterism. By twenty-three, I'd mined all the profundity to be had from *I'm the only Black guy here*. It also wasn't that the crowds at each event were like each other. Any of the Latin whites from Miami or the Brooklyn Jews would have been as conspicuous a presence in this chapel as I was at all three gatherings. The disquieting detail was that they were, by every conceivable measure, interchangeable. Thoroughbreds. Made of all the same stuff.

How envious I felt! All the privilege that lived there—the privilege to construct a universe in their own image, or perhaps to be molded by a universe that had an image for them in mind. From their earliest days, they'd been provided a North Star and were shepherded along its trail. There must, I imagine, be a much clearer path to Self when one's community is a pressure cooker. They nodded *yes* to the selves they'd eventually become while still in the cradle. Did they know the good fortune they'd happened upon?

Despite our shared adolescences, the ones who were my age strode through life so differently than I. They walked with the certainty belonging breeds. I recalled my years of misfittedness back home, those years when a sense of self always felt just beyond my reach. I looked at them gathered in the pews and thought *no shit.* How thick must I have been to ever think us alike. So much difference stretched between my community and me. It saturated the clothes I wore, the dialects I spoke, the flashing billboard of difference that wrapped my frame. They could look to each other for affirmation. Every interaction, whether in congeniality or contest, reassured them of their normalcy.

I was tempted to deem this comfort they enjoyed *white privilege*, until I remembered the day we laid Pop to rest. A different village came together then, one as far-removed from the Cliftons as Memphis to Mallorca. There, too, I gazed from an altar and viewed a world unto its own, though I didn't then recognize it as such, perhaps because I looked more at home within it. But I see it now. The *Sirs* and the *Ma'ams*, the *Amen*s and the *Mhmms*, their customs had rhythm. There was no denying the culture from whence they came and would remain. For them too, the universe provided anchoring.

But could this privilege, I wondered, be a gift to them all? Or were there those for whom the anchor was a weight, and the privilege, a straitjacket? Surely there were boys and girls who wriggled and writhed in their Sunday's best, feeling there were other identities out there better tailored to their types. They must be in the crowd, cloaked in the signals of their belonging, victims to the privilege they neither asked for nor wanted. What of the ones who smalled themselves to conform?

Mr. Clifton embodied his world's archetype. Even I saw in

him a silhouette I once hoped to fill out. Dozens of young ones were pressed from his mold, just as he himself must've been shaped, until he inhabited the role flawlessly. He was so seemingly secure, a keystone to that arch that fit snugly and *just so*. But if I am to consider Mr. Clifton's embrace of life's beginning and middle, I must also consider his rejection at its end. Mr. Clifton was a paragon; and when a paragon falls, he forces one to wonder whether the blessing of belonging had always been so sweet, or if the weight of that life he projected caused his crumble.

And if belonging and certainty can prove toxic, then maybe betweenness has its own set of privileges as well. Maybe, like the congregation, I overlooked my privilege, taking it for granted through years of bitching and itchy skin. For my difference was unavoidable—it loomed large. It couldn't be buried beneath gilded snaps or lily whites. I couldn't tamp it down and walk around with weighted spirit, if I so chose. Its very obviousness meant that one day, inevitably, I would learn to negotiate it. Yes, it required years of grappling, stumbling, trial and error, but I confronted it head-on. I had to. Unbeknown to them, that congregation demanded it. As did my parents, and teachers; Martha's Vineyard and the Black Table; Willow and Cara and Anna; and the whole wide world around us all. And after those years, I freed its grip. My difference did not crush me.

There's privilege in fighting for, and achieving, deliverance.

In the midst of that wrestling match called *growing up*, another gift manifested, one I only later recognized. For, though there was discomfort in the absence of a single self, there is privilege in learning to forge a home in the many, in identifying that which is more valuable even than culture. Without a clear universe to claim, I embarked upon the project of erecting my own community, thieving tidbits from other universes I passed through along the way. Grey folk must learn to look far and wide in search of Self, far enough to understand that the borders of the comfortable encircle a playpen. We find our way in a greater expanse.

The jury is out on marriage, but I will certainly one day die. My body will wilt, and my mind, if blessed, will season the way old, cast-iron pans do. If I do it as I intend, I'll greet my end with restraint. I won't greedily grasp for more seconds. I'll look my creator in the eye and decide. And then, it will be done. I find a great dignity in not clinging to life so closely that you allow it to twist you, instead floating over to the other side with nothing but a soft smile and gratitude.

If I am the man I hope to be on the day before that day (so many ifs), I will leave behind my own chapel of mournful, joyous souls. And whether from above or below, I will look to them and see a broader swath of this earth than many ever get to intimately know. Thriving in the betweenness means crossing the cultural paltriness others mistake for palisades. My village will have been fastened together from the card-carrying members of other villages and I will feel privileged to call that mosaic my own.

The all of me will be present in the all of them, just as it is for all others—just as it was for Mr. Clifton.

That's the idea anyway.

CLOSING

I WAS A JUNIOR at Georgetown when this project began. The scent of high school still faintly clung to me but had largely faded away. Along with it, the arrogance, the remnants of senior year king-of-the-heap-ism. I'd reached the midpoint of collegiate life and had been pummeled from the stratosphere. I inched toward a realization that college was not so good at teaching but adept at illuminating the never-ending breadth of my own unknowing. I'd come in as a finance major, prepared to claw and 'bow for a Goldman Sachs' berth with the rest of the hair-gelled lot. Two years in, I was drifting between the humanities. My classmates had Tibetan tattoos and an opinion on the plight of Burma. Then seemed as good a time as any to look back; to assess that which made me and to consider what it'd made.

I embarked on a semester-long project then that, nearly four years on, hadn't reached a natural end. Growth is understood retrospectively; it's hard to comprehend from the center. I considered, wrote, reconsidered, rewrote, and repeated until insanity darkened my door. Then I finished or stopped.

Today, I'm something that resembles something that looks like a full-grown man, if you squint your eyes and tilt your head just so. A few years and a few hundred thousand words spilt has brought me to precious few conclusions. And a well of gratitude. The adolescent process of figuring out has proven worthwhile. The hardest lessons learned back in Philly were crystalized in university and still carry me through these early years of grown-up life.

That ambivalence that I sat with for years as a young one was converted into something more productive in college. D.C. was so much bigger than the home I'd come to know. My Philly was a Black and white thing; a rich, and blue-collar, and broke as a joke thing. The lines were clear.

Georgetown was different; it introduced me to people who were grey in their own, novel ways. The Indian daughter of a beverage executive and her roommate, a half-Swedish, half-Egyptian girl, both raised in London. There was the Persian Angeleno, the Ghanaian economist, and the ostentatious son of a Nigerian banker—all friends. My first roommate was a Chinese American, Tea Party Republican from Long Island. Other New Yorkers followed him, as did an English exchange student, a Korean jackass who lived in Hong Kong, and a half-Indian leftist raised between Bangalore and Connecticut.

An economy of intrigue mounted around their quilted back-grounds. It wasn't enough to be engaging; multiculturalism had to be branded across the forehead. *So American* was epithetic. The mundane inverted to the peculiar and vice versa—Span-iards and Arabs ogled our Arkansan friend like he was Mar-tian. By second semester I learned not to begin conversations with *where are you from?* unless I was interested in enduring the fifteen-minute explanation that might follow.

Grey was in.

There were drawbacks, of course. Elitism eventually fol-lowed. As did the siloing of certain groups by language family, or region of origin, or drug of choice. That was, however, the safe move. It was possible to stand at the front gates and witness the unknown world stretch in every direction. Opting for the familiar would've brought comfort, and a shortchanging of Self.

To thrive in that environment, to cross-cultural cliques and find friends in the many, one had to know how to navigate the in-between. One needed to balance panderage and chauvinism and strike dead center; to be all things without losing one's essence.

It was as though I'd practiced on purpose.

Those same qualities that pushed between Philly and me drew Georgetown in close. I discovered a new confidence, root-ed in truth rather than hot air. I was equal parts Black Table shit talk and Hoosier sensibility; Ethiopian will and Hiller assur-ance. I was part whatever they'd left me with too, the jumbled Georgetown bevy. I was all Black. I learned to be all things at once. I learned to take pride in my mix. People still told me, in the latter years, from time to time, what I wasn't. *Oh well,* I thought. Sometimes I spoke out, sometimes I didn't. It was only ever a question of pragmatism. I knew what I was.

Then it was once again time to uproot. Graduation came and with it the promise of a perilous world beyond—a new phase full of its own firsts. I poked my head out timidly. Indeed, adulting has been like running with scissors. Or maybe, like a chicken whose head has been cutoff running with scissors. I will be greatly indebted to the person who finally explains to me taxes and 401(k) contributions. A degree in Justice and Peace Studies does wonders for the abstract and very little for the particular.

There are other challenges—anxieties and apprehensions, shackles and spurs—that run deeper as well. It seems I've traded insecurities of the self for insecurities of the future. There is a constant *what the fuck am I doing?* smog floating above all. Uncertainty pours into the lungs and stops my breath short. But that's growing up, I suppose.

It's hardly all bad. This part of life presents new freedoms as well—chief among them, the freedom to surround myself with only that which I deem important. I've begun to construct a universe of my own, not unlike Pop and Mr. Clifton; it's the same freedom Jackson stumbled upon during his first summer in New York. Much of my time is my own; juvenile pressures don't determine how it's spent. I do.

I have been blessed to encounter myriad intelligent, kindhearted people (who have little else in the way of commonality) to bring into my fold, and I theirs—many still around from

Philly, most from the time since matriculation. I run with a crowd less committed to their preconceptions. They are phenomenally unprejudiced and, by and large, they get me. That may be a sign of the times or our increasing maturity. It may be, as I suggest, selection bias. Whatever the case, it works.

That is, however, only part of this new life. Alas, some of my time, in recent months, has not been my time. Some of my time has belonged to The Man. Following graduation, I packed up my belongings and flew to Chicago to peddle software for a tech giant. That lasted eight months. Like the finance major, my role in corporate life was assumed rather than sprung for, and wrongly so. On quitting day, a coworker, herself Black, approached me: *Three of the Black people in our program are leaving. I'm going to say something. There must be a cultural problem that needs addressing.* East Coasters made similar points of Chicago broadly, which in their Manhattan-centric model of the universe, registered as a blip just off the Oregon Trail. *Ain't they racist at your job?*

To them all, I was conflicted.

On the one hand, of course ignorance abounded. It was a more subdued thing, absent the adolescent animus I'd grown to know (kids can be so mean), but present nonetheless. I did, with spotty regularity, come to see how office ignorance operated, even in the utopian town of tech. I was called out of my name more than once, given look-alikes I didn't look like. Things that, in my experience, registered as *the small stuff*.

Token times proved instructive. Life as the only teaches one to parse the ignorance of the ill-informed from the ignorance of the malicious. And, hopefully, to curtail the power of those microaggressions that comprise the former. My body formed a resistance; it callused over old scrapes. Slights at the proverbial watercooler got an empty grin and a nod, then slipped away like wet soap.[18]

Not only did I learn to cope with backwardness, I even, strangely, learned to see past it. I learnt to disentangle the traits that were good in a person, and if not good, *useful*, from the prejudiced parts, even while acknowledging that those same people may not see me at all, my good or my less-than. It was an act of self-preservation, not blind optimism. Racism and its lesser cousins were too pervasive to think otherwise. I didn't want to look to all sides with loathing and suspicion. I chose hope instead.

I tell a version of that view to some friends and receive puzzlement. Worse, from others, I get scornful glances in return, as though I have called *uncle* to the whims of the white world. What I call hope, they dub denial. People I keep close, people whose judgement I lean on, they tell me how real they'd keep it if they were me. One hundred fifty percent real. I question if what I've come to is not just weakness, betrayal even, euphemized for my own pacification. But then I'm reminded of so many I know who shake their fists at the whiteness they encounter and stew in disappoint thereafter. Talented folk who clip their own wings rather than toddle into tokenhood for fear of what they might find there.

---

18 We didn't have a literal water cooler. I got my water from the espresso bar on our floor, along with my matcha.

I haven't let this white world abase my Black. I've just refused to let it madden me. I've staked my peace within it, like a
towel on a crowded beach. That, I've come to decide, is the most
crucial freedom of all—peace in a place that conspires against
your sanity. I've exchanged a lifetime, so far, for the peace I steep
in. I ain't lettin' it go for nothin'.

Afterword
COLE WORLD
(OR, WHAT CAN BROWN DO FOR YOU?)

by Michael Eric Dyson

THE IMAGE ARRESTS ME of a tall, wispy, beautiful boy, intense and serious, smart as all get out, confident yet not conceited, humble enough to recognize his need to learn and grow as he eagerly embraced a curiosity about the world that was nearly all-consuming. I was good friends with his old man, whose pride in his son, whose enormous desire for him to find his place in the world, prompted me and Cole to exchange emails as he sought admission to Georgetown. I realized quickly he had the goods, and when, of course, he earned a place in school and took my courses, I learned firsthand he had a sharp intellect.

But like you, gentle reader, there's so much I've discovered about him in these eloquent pages full of gorgeous prose. I had no idea of all that he had been through: The bruising racial encounters on soccer fields. The searing vulnerabilities announced when police brutality reared its ugly head, yet again. The child-hood griefs and glories. The unavoidable, yet highly instructive, at least in his hands, trials and tribulations of the artist as a young man. And the pleasures and perils of self-discovery that await a kid whose parent's unmixed love offered a potent mix of passion and reason to a child who went forth into a mixed-up world. It was a world that wouldn't always endorse his dogged hopefulness about our common fate in a country going happily to hell in a handbasket of its own making. But that's where we are.

Cole's reveal, and what's more, his big reveal—the acknowl-edgment that the sheltered world that love gave to him was often shattered by too many folks' fatal ignorance of race and still others' joyful obliviousness to the humanity that black folk should by now be able to take for granted, but sadly, still can't—prompt us to consider what's been revealed to us since Donald Trump took office. This isn't quite a Book of Revelations. But Cole is at times a scribe exiled on an island of good sense as he prophesies about racial confusion and political corruption. John the Baptist meet Cole the Blended.

The last four years since Trump took office have been an absolute nightmare for those who treasure truth, who treasure science, who treasure facts, who treasure love, kindness, and compassion, who, honestly, treasure democracy. Of course, we were not perfect before his rise. We didn't sing Kumbaya every day and wish everyone goodnight like we were the Waltons. We were under siege by the deals that neoliberalism cut with big business as we bailed out big corporations but left the little guys to fend for themselves. We fought bigotry under a black president mostly by ignoring it and wishing it would go away. But it didn't. It got suspended from class but came back as a bully to menace the schoolyard.

The eight-year presidency of a black man with a white mother and African father can't be taken lightly in the equation. To those who had waited a lifetime to see the dawning of a new day of American promise in full color, Obama's presidency was a sort of racial nirvana. But it quickly shifted to the revelation of another side of the American people. It was a dark and foreboding place where Fox News levels of black antipathy combusted in every political nook and social cranny. Barack's blackness exploded more inside the fretful imaginations of fearful bigots than it did on the frontlines of black politics. He was a decidedly moderate politician. His modest goals got read as progressive by charitable supporters. His sworn enemies tagged him as a left-wing radical. Obama barely stood a chance in many quarters of the culture that didn't cotton to a black man telling them anything about anything. As much enthusiasm as he generated among some white folk, he provoked profound anxiety in many others. And in some cases, that fear transmogrified into outright hatred. Many saw Obama as an existential threat to the American way of life. His dangerous blackness had to be removed at all costs.

Obama was opposed by an unwieldy gaggle of birthers, deep-state conspirators, neofascist zealots, neo-Nazi advocates, and rabid white supremacists. Their symbolic leader was, and remains, Donald Trump. Of course, he's not technically any of those things. He hasn't officially signed on to any of their camps. But he indulges in the politics of implication, coding, signifying, symbolizing, and adroit suggestion. He leaves the ideological defense of such nefarious beliefs to hardliners as he goes about governing. But he keeps an ear to their venomous ground and an eye on their spiraling smoke signals. If he can't say it outright, he can at least support ideas, beliefs, passions, and visions that are driven by the denizens of a claustrophobic nostalgia. They seek to restore the country to its former glory after being knocked off their square. They are the purveyors of reactionary whiteness in the face of dangerous blackness.

Donald Trump's reactionary whiteness gained metaphysical currency when he darkened the Oval Office. It got a boost into triumphant whiteness when his election cloaked him in troubling legitimacy. White nationalists were giddy and gleeful that one of their own snagged a seat of ultimate power. It made little difference that he was one of them more by instinct and outlook than ideology or true belief. They were ecstatic that he managed to displace the pathological blackness that had preceded him. He immediately set out to destroy every remnant and measure of Obama's presence, to erase every policy and public pronouncement. The coin of his realm is racial animus, racial hostility, and racial resentment. At the same time he cries out as a victim of liberal and progressive forces which he claims to be anti-American. The alchemy of white grievance turns white bigotry into loyalty to the nation. It asserts white nationalism the premise of true American democracy.

Donald Trump is the symbol of malevolent whiteness come to monstrous life. He is oblivious to white privilege, indifferent to compassion, and hostile to self-reflection. A malignant narcissism claims his every waking moment as he seeks to spot his face in each issue with which the nation struggles. The devotees of Trump's triumphant whiteness fantasize him riding in on a white horse to save the world. He bullies foreign leaders. He is vindictive to domestic rivals and allies. He is churlish to ordinary citizens and celebrities alike who dare chastise his vicious behavior. And he has tragically given the green light to alt-right groups to spew racist bile as they find refuge and comfort in the Oval Office. Trump employs white nationalist Stephen Miller as an advisor. The well of ideas Trump draws from is poisoned by the hate of black folk and other people of color.

Donald Trump's presidency mocks the best values of our democracy. His leadership growth is gravely stunted. He refuses to listen to reason. He fails to reckon with opposing arguments. He cannot hear any truth outside his echo chamber. He can't help but offer flat and false interpretations of American history. He is in many ways a threat to national security. Perhaps some white folk who have been blind to their own white identities see reflected in Trump the fatal consequences of whiteness. Perhaps they will finally see that whiteness is often a cover for harmful beliefs and behaviors. The revelation of the Trump years is that when white racial immaturity is weaponized it sinks the national fate and attacks our collective soul.

The only way out is to tell the truth about what it means to be black, white, both, neither, red, brown, yellow, or any other color or combination. It should be apparent from this book that we conjure race in part from our social imaginations. It is supported by logic and the cultural forms to which it gives rise. This permits us to see how Trump's implacable white grievance keeps him addressing racial inequalities and social inequities. It means being honest about how his support ranges far beyond the poor and working white classes. It extends to those with plenty of bank and business. It means acknowledging that many white folks are quite willing to look the other way as Trump vilifies black folk as long as their own cupboards are stocked and their bellies are full. It means admitting that armed white folk protested state closings and flooded the streets once it became apparent that the novel coronavirus pandemic affected black folk in far more deadly fashion. And Trump was equally tone-deaf when the plague of police brutality revealed its mortal persistence. When a cop suffocated forty-six-year-old George Floyd with his knee, and protesters took to the streets, the president, who enthusiastically supported the angry white mobs protesting state closings, lit into the angry protests over Floyd's killing.

We need Cole's story. Only when we grapple with the telling nuances, and with the explicit expressions, too, of a complicated racial identity like his can we resist Trump's distorted vision of America. The real revelation here is Cole Brown. He is a budding literary star with the intellectual chops to match his moral ambition. Let's applaud his vital momentum and wish him well as he explores his gift to make us see the truth in full color.

ACKNOWLEDGMENTS

THERE'S A LONG LIST of people who brought this project to life, and to them, I owe the world.

Mama first. Upon completion of the writing process, it occurred to me that I had inadvertently placed myself in an uncomfortable conundrum. When I began, some four years ago, I did not set out to write a memoir. I wanted this book to first and foremost deal with the subject matter: the lives of tokens. To that end, I added my own stories where I thought them pertinent, but always with a mind to the bigger picture. The resulting work, I have found, is one that, if read incorrectly, would suggest some untruths about those I hold most dear. There are a few people who have an outsized presence in the book incommensurate with their status of little import in my heart. Of course, the reverse rings true as well, and chief among these underserved minor characters is my mother. She is power and grace embodied. I am never as acutely aware of my limitations as a writer as when meditating on the words befitting her role in my own life and the lives of countless others to whom I have watched her give so selflessly. Adequate adjectives have eluded me in the past as it appears they are now. I will leave it at a simple, woefully insufficient sentiment: I am me because you are you. Thank you. I love you with every fiber of my being.

Faith, as she will be quick to remind me, did not get nearly enough shine either. She's my soldier. I look at her and am reminded of all my many shortcomings. I did the best I could to be a strong male presence, which was not nearly good enough, but whether because of or in spite of having me around, she has become a remarkable, tough, principled, fashionable, talented, opinionated—did I mention fashionable?—caring, beautiful juggernaut of a young woman. I couldn't be prouder.

Thank you to the teachers I've had who got me to stop chatting up girls long enough to poke my nose in a book or two. Ms. Allen, Ms. Waleson, Mrs. Walker, Mrs. Jacoby, Mrs. Aldridge, Mrs. Jones, and Ms. Moses—you all are the teachers who young children dream of becoming. A special shoutout goes to Mr. Dziedzic, who let me sit in his office and bicker over Ralph Ellison and Dostoevsky until long after duty required; and Professor Norma Tilden, who showed me the weight of an article. Extra special shoutout goes to Professor Eric Koester, who made me sit down and start writing this thing. He never asked if I had a book in me, he just pointed to a laptop and told me to write until one appeared. I needed that.

Acknowledgments

Thank you to the friends who took time out of busy schedules to drudge up awkward high school encounters for no reason other than the call of their generous spirits. There were too many stories to include in this book but know that the final product couldn't have come together without the input of each and every one of you. Earl, Kobby, Corbin, Blake, Jackson, Amira, Sophia, Jamie, Maya, Sebastian, Veronica, Trey—you're all rock stars. I must also mention Ben, Kyra, Daryl, Andreea, and Devon, who are my closest ties on this earth and, like Mama and Faith, did not get the attention they deserved in this forum.

Thank you to the literary pros who shepherded me through this years-long process, particularly the good folks at Skyhorse, Rebecca Shoenthal and Hector Carosso most of all. Thank you, Armstrong Williams, for bringing me to them. Thanks also to the long list of people who took early looks at the rough-cut manuscript, helping me to convert sporadic, often incoherent ideas into the book you're holding: Billy Whitaker, Shanna Milkey, Graham Thorburn for their edits, and Sarah Metz, Anthony Rodriguez, Elaine Welteroth, plus many others for their unfiltered opinions.

Thank you, Natalie Johnson, artist extraordinaire. What a beautiful series of masterpieces you've created.

Thank you, Mr. Andre Harrell, for your time and wisdom. I wish I could've shown you where things ended up. I'll be sure to bring a copy with me when we meet again.

Thank you, D'Angelo, Amy Winehouse, Dave East, Miles

Davis, Jorja Smith, Dreamville, and Fela Kuti for creating songs to write to.

Thank you, Ta-Nehisi Coates, who gripped me by my sides and rolled me around as a college sophomore and who, in the most private of moments that allow my imagination to unfurl, I fantasize of being half as good as someday. And also my sociology professor, Dr. Michael Eric Dyson, whose lectures came in a bastardized vernacular of Detroit slang and SAT vocabulary that granted new meaning to the term eloquence. I emulate it whenever possible.

Finally, I do owe a debt of sorts to my father, Payne Brown. Through both his presence and absence, I grew conscious. I know many who stumble through life sleepily or plunge their heads into the sand at low tide. The call of their hazy perception startles me more than the grave. I'm glad I ain't them.

I will exit as I arrived—thanks Ma.